# Orchids of India – III
# Biodiversity and Status of *Vanda* Jones ex R. Br.

# Orchids of India – III Biodiversity and Status of *Vanda* Jones ex R. Br.

**Limasenla,**
**Yogendra Kumar**
Botany Dcpartment
North-Eastern Hill University
Shillong - 793022, India
&
**Jauti Sharma**
Botany Department
St. Anthony's College,
Shillong - 793001, India

**2002**

**Daya Publishing House**
**Delhi - 110 035**

ISBN 81-7035-238-X



*Published by* : **Daya Publishing House**
1123/74, Deva Ram Park,
Tri Nagar, Delhi - 110 035
Phone : 7103999
Fax : (011) 7199029
e-mail : dayabooks@vsnl.com
website : www.dayabooks.com

*Showroom* : 4762-63/23, Ansari Road, Darya Ganj,
New Delhi - 110002
Phone: 3245578, 3244987

*Laser Typesetting* : **Classic Computer Services**
Delhi - 110 035

*Printed at* : **Chawla Offset Printers**
Delhi - 110 052

PRINTED IN INDIA

# Acknowledgement

We would like to thank The Head, Department of Botany, NEHU & DBT, for providing all the facilities required for research.

An unending list of friends and colleagues had encouraged us in innumerable ways. We take this opportunity to express our heartfelt gratitude to each and every one of them.

Last but not the least, we are deeply indebted to our parents and family members for their moral support and encouragement.

**— Authors**

# Contents

# Contents

# List of Plates, Tables & Figures

**Conclusion**

# Chapter 1
# Introduction

Plant taxonomy is the basis to other fields of plant sciences and simultaneously dependent on them even with recent advancement and increase in our understanding of the subject, knowledge is not complete until the data form all other fields of investigation have been incorporated. According to Stace (1989), any data that show differences from species to species and within species are of taxonomic significance, and thus constitute part of the information or evidence that may be used by the taxonomist. Therefore, it is desirable that a wide range of information from diverse sources should be used to obtain the best sort of natural or phenetic classification.

Modern trends in taxonomy or experimental taxonomy have been emphasised by different workers (Radford *et al.*, 1974; Davis and Heywood, 1963; Benson, 1962; Sneath and Sokal, 1973). However, the ultimate objectives remain almost the same. It involves accumulation of data from various fields like morphology, anatomy, cytology, palynology, genetics, seed morphometry, embryology, physiology, ecology etc. Advanced genetics, breeding, biotechnology and pharmaceutical sciences have to be backed by advanced taxonomy. Khoshoo (1995) has emphasised on the importance of taxonomy in the light of recent biodiversity convention. Conservation biology is becoming a very important field and taxonomy is the first and foremost discipline which plays an important role in this field of study.

A comprehensive knowledge of the taxa from various aspects become very essential for the appropriate placement of taxa in the taxonomic system. The morphological approach has certainly provided a workable system, but the modern trend in taxonomy has contributed information on the applicability of data from various disciplines. Consequently, taxonomy, which has become the most dynamic discipline, particularly during the last three decades, has not only provided the classification based on synthetic theory but also revealed the mechanism of evolution at various levels of taxonomic hierarchy.

The family orchidaceae is one of the most widespread amongst all the families of flowering plants. On the evolutionary scale, orchids are considered as the most advanced group. Their flowers exhibit extremely diverse variety of shapes, sizes, colours and fragrances in their bizarre floral makeup. No other decorative plants can surpass the beauty and persistency of the orchid flowers. According to various assessments, the orchids with more than 20,000 species under about 800 genera are found to occur all over the world; exception being, perhaps in the polar regions (Garay, 1960; Schulter and Pease, 1963; Arditti, 1979; Dressler, 1981; Alberto and Rossi, 1988; Chadha, 1992 and Peter, 1994). The orchids include taxa of epiphytic, lithophytic, terrestrial and saprophytic habit. India with it's 3.29 million sq. km of geographic area 7,000 km of coastline is assumed to posses approximately 1,300 species belonging to about 160 genera (Arora and Mukherjee, 1983; Jain and Mehrotra, 1984; Manilal and Kumar, 1986; Chadha, 1992). The orchidaceae is the second largest family of flowering plants in India. However, an exact estimate of the total orchid wealth in the country awaits botanical exploration in several virgin forests. More recently the occurrence of 1,141 species in 166 genera representing all the major orchid tribes – Apostasieae, Cypripedieae, Neottieae, Orchideae and Epidendreae have been listed by Sathish Kumar and Manilal (1994). Nearly 60 percent of these species are epiphytic in habit. The country has been an active centre of speciation and species diversification has been at its maximum in the Himalayan and the Northeastern regions, whereas endemism has been more pronounced in the peninsular regions (Vij, 1998). The Indian subcontinent is also considered as a primary or secondary source of origin of the orchids. Majority of Indian orchids are concentrated in the phytogeographically interesting North–East India, with about 700 species (Kataki *et al*, 1984; Hegde, 1987a; Kumar *et al*, 1994). This region is rich in orchid taxa that grows in profusion, endowed with highest ornamental value (Kumar and Sharma, 1992).

The genus *Vanda* of orchidaceae family is one of the most popular groups of orchids both between hobbyist and commercial growers (Hegde, 1984). No other genus of large flowered orchids display the diversity of colours and pattern that modern *Vanda* do (Martin, 1988). A well grown strap–leaved *Vanda* is a majestic specimen, leaves neatly and regularly arranged in a fish–bone pattern. *Vanda* forms some of the most magnificent orchids that India in general and North–Eastern region in particular can boast about (Sharma and Kumar, 1993).

This monopodial group belongs to the sub family orchidoideae, tribe Epidendreae and sub tribe Sarcanthinae (True– *Vanda*). The *Vanda* group is an Indo–Malayan genus extending from India to South–East Asia, Borneo, Indonesia, Papua, New Guinea and North Australia with about forty species. India is one of the major natural habitats of *Vanda* in the world with thirteen species. However, the ruthless exploitation and their habitat destruction have brought a number of species on the verge of extinction. Taxonomy of *Vanda* is complex and difficult. There are attempts to transfer some of the *Vanda* species to other existing genera and also erection of new genera, e.g. *Taprobanea* Christ., *Trudelia* Garay and *Euanthe* Schltr. for some species of *Vanda*. No comprehensive account of Indian *Vandas* exist except lists of orchidaceous members which has included eleven species of *Vanda* by Pradhan (1979) nine species by Jain and Mehrotra (1984), ten species by Kartikeyan *et al.* (1989). Therefore, it becomes important and necessary to update and prepare a revisionary account of Indian *Vanda*.

Biodiversity, which is the total variability within a taxon and within a species, often termed "gene bank" is important for improvement of certain varieties through breeding programs. The rich biodiversity of the *Vanda* is extremely important, both horticulturally and medicinally. The medicinal value of *Vanda*ceous taxon has been discussed in "Charaka Samhita" – an ancient Indian medicinal treatise written by Charaka in Sanskrit a few thousand years ago. This forms the first record of Indian orchids in Ayurveda. The genus *Vanda* is striking in the sense that they feature great variation of colours, tessellation–pattern, shapes and sizes observable within the different species. This renders the group a major priority for both the orchidologist and also the floriculturist. Perusal of literature reveals that this aspect is less attempted for a complete taxon in orchidaceae. Therefore, the present study deals with the Indian species of *Vanda*.

Plant phenology or chronological study refers to seasonal patterns of leafing, flowering, fruiting, dehiscence etc. of a given species in different seasons. Observations on different phenophases are important in germplasm collection and also for the better understanding of the ecological adaptations of individual species and interactions (Stern and Rochi, 1974). In orchids, the calender of flowering and fruiting varies from species to species. The genus *Vanda* are horticulturally important which has produced spectacular hybrids in the past few decades. Therefore, it is important to study the phenological events not only to understand the ecological adaptation of each species but also to provide an information in the conservation of the species. As there is no comprehensive data on Indian *Vandas*, the present work has included this aspect with regard to the Indian species of *Vanda*.

The morphological characters of pollen grains and spores are important diagnostic criteria in consideration of the taxonomy and interrelationships of plants at various taxonomic levels (Nair, 1985). Orchids are the only group that contains a great diversity in their pollen association from primitive diandrous species with monads, to the more advanced monadrous orchids showing tetrads, massulae or pollinia (Kapil and Arora, 1990). The present century has made rapid progress in the field of palynology. Nevertheless, concerning Indian orchids, data are scanty except Chardard, 1971; Vij and Kashyap, 1978; Newton and Willams, 1978; Arora, 1985, Arora and Kapil, 1989; Joy, 1992. The palynology of Indian orchids seems to be one of the least studied fields. Apart from some stray papers, no comprehensive work has been done in India in this subject (Manilal and Satish Kumar, 1986). Therefore, the present work tried to provided a consolidate account on Indian species of *Vanda*.

Morphometric studies of orchid seeds can be useful in solving both taxonomic and phylogenetic problems and may also explain some important aspects on seed biology (Barthlott, 1976; Arditti *et al.*, 1979; Patrick *et al.*, 1980; Joy *et al.*, 1994). Orchid seeds are the smallest among those produced by the flowering plants and vary considerably in size, morphology, colour, structure and the fine details. In general, only few studies on orchid seed morphometry are available (Barthlott, 1976; Arditti *et al.*, 1980; Patrick *et al.*, 1980). In view of the important role of this aspect contributing to both academic and applied value, the present work has investigated the seed morphometry of Indian species of *Vanda*.

The importance of cytology in clarifying taxonomy and evolution of orchid species has been established by various workers. Karasawa and Saito (1982) suggested that chromosome number and karyotype are taxonomically useful. Even in species with the same chromosome number the karyotypes are distinctive. Cytological data of the *Vanda*ceous group have been extensively accumulated mostly from North–Eastern Himalayas and Southern India, however a comprehensive work including karyotype analysis is lacking. According to the reports available the number of chromosomes seem to vary in some species, despite the fact that the basic number being uniform within the genus. Therefore, the investigators made an attempt to study the basic chromosome number along with a thorough karyotype study in Indian species of *Vanda*.

Thus, the present work investigated the following aspects viz; Biodiversity, Phenology, Palynology, Seed morphometry and Cytology pertaining to the following species of *Vanda namely; V.alpina, V.bicolor, V.coerulea, V.coerulescens, V.cristata, V. liouvillei, V.pumila, V.stangeana, V. tessellata, and V. testacea.*

The above mentioned aspects of experimental taxonomy undertaken in the present work would define a systematic relationship of the taxon and also facilitate more information in the field of germplasm conservation. This work has also highlighted a better prospect for scientific multiplication and utilization of the potential resource of Indian species of *Vanda*.

# Chapter 2
# Review of Literature

This chapter presents a review of the literatures related to the present study under the following aspects.

**Biodiversity**: Biodiversity is the basic requirement to progress for improving productivity of plants, animals and all living organisms for the survival of human beings on the earth. The conservation of biodiversity has received considerable attention all over the world since the convention on biological diversity signed by 170 countries at Rio De Janeiro in June 1992, and has come into force from 29th December 1993.

The concept of biological diversity has been emphasized variously among the scientific communities. Wilcox (1984) has defined it as the variety of life forms in a given region, the ecological roles they perform and the genetic diversity they contain. Another comprehensive definition is provided by Reid & Miller (1989), according to them, "Biodiversity is the variety of world's organisms, including their genetic diversity and the assemblages they form". Khoshoo (1996) has also defined it as – the total sum of plants and animals (including human beings) and micro organisms existing as an interacting system in the biosphere.

Generally biodiversity is described in terms of genes, species and ecosystems. As genes are the components of species, and species are the components of ecosystems, species richness is central to the concept of biodiversity (Ravi and Pushpangadan, 1996).

In a series of recent papers, strategies on biodiversity conservation has been discussed (Khoshoo, 1996; Charles, 1996; Heywood, 1996; Damodaran, 1996). Rao (1986) has highlighted the floristic diversity of eastern Himalayas. In 1998, he also presented an informative article on the biodiversity of Northeast India.

Numerical diversity of orchids has been assessed by various workers. According to them, the orchids have more than 20,000 species under about 800 genera (Garey, 1960; Schulter & Pease, 1963; Dressler, 1981; Alberto & Rossi, 1988; Chadha, 1992; Peter, 1994). The orchidaceae is the second largest family of flowering plants in India (Rao, 19866). The number of Indian orchids are reported to be 1,300 species approximately. Out of these, 750 species are reported in Northeast region of India (Manilal & Kumar, 1986; Karthikeyan *et al.*, 1989; Sharma, 1993; Kumar *et al.*, 1994).

The contributions made on the rich orchid wealth of northeast region are those of Pradhan (1979), Hegde (1984), Kataki (1986) and Chankija *et al.* (1992). Besides sporadic reports and accounts are also available by many workers (Jain & Hajra, 1976; Verma & Sharma, 1976; Deb, 1983; Arora & Mukherjee, 1983; Rao, 1986. Ghatak & Devi, 1988; Kataki & Hynniewta, 1986; Hegde, 1987; Kumar & Sharma, 1992, 1993).

General accounts and occurrence of the genus *Vanda* has been dealt by authors like Seidenfaden (1988, 1992), Cheng & Tand (1988). There are also scattered accounts on *Vanda* in states/regional and national orchid floras such as King & Pantling (1898), Abraham & Vatsala (1981), Bose and Battacharji (1980), Kataki (1984), Jain & Mehrotra (1984), Karthikeyan *et al* (1989), Maheshwari (1995).

From the literatures available it appears that almost all the species of *Vanda* are important in floriculture which has produced spectacular hybrids in the past few decades. Out of 40 species in the genus, India is one of the major natural habitats of *Vanda* (Kumar *et al.*, 1997). But the rich genetic diversity of plant species including orchids is being depleted, and many species are facing threat in their natural habitat as advocated by Jain & Sastry (1980), Sastry *et al.* (1983), Haridasan & Rao (1985), Nair & Sastry (1988 – 1990). Therefore, it is important to establish a complete revisionary account on Indian *Vanda*s.

**Phenology**: Plant phenology which deals with the seasonal patterns of leaf sprouting and development, flowering and anthesis, fruit setting, development and retention, and leaf and fruit drop has been discussed by Lawrence (1955), Opler *et al.* (1980), Ralhan *et al.* (1985), Rawal *et al.* (1991). These specified events has been a topic of scientific study since the 19th century (Aitken, 1974). It is of great interest in agriculture where the timing of flower and fruit determines the crop yield (White, 1997; Loomies & Connor, 1992).

The concept and significance of phenological studies has been discussed by Leith (1970) and Leith & Radford (1971). The importance of phenological study in germplasm collection and ecological adaptations of individual species and their interactions has been emphasised by Stern & Rochi (1974), Waser (1979), Thompsom (1980).

Different workers have different views regarding the reproductive phenophases in plants. Janzen (1967) regarded sexual selection as the ultimate cause and environmental triggers as the proximate cause. While Simpson (1977), Solbrig & Yang (1977) suggested high soil moisture as the determinant in flowering of tree species. On the other hand, Waser (1979) and Thompson (1980) suggested pollinator availability for flowering phenology.

The flowering triggers for a number of plants are known (Jakson, 1966) crop and ornamental plants (Caprio, 1973, Wielzolaski, 1973). Studies have shown that certain species may have greater variation in phenological events as a result of intra specific genetic variation rather than environmental differences (Mc.Millan, 1957; Mc.Millan & Pagel, 1958; Vance & Kucera, 1960; Gilbert, 1961).

In India phenological studies on tree species was conducted by a number of workers (Krishnaswamy & Mathuda, 1954; Kaul & Raina, 1980; Ralhan *et al.*, 1985;

Nasari & Bhadola, 1989; Vinayan & Kumbhojkar, 1991; Rawal *et al.*, 1991; Bhat, 1992; Semalty & Sharma, 1996).

With respect to phenology of orchids, Vander Pijl & Dodson (1966) has emphasised on the orchid flower, pollination and evolution. Nilsson (1978) worked on pollination ecology and adaptations. Similarly Javier *et al.* (1992), Kim *et al.* (1994) and Sabat & Ackerman (1996) focused their work on flowering phenology and pollinator availability. Benzing and Atwood (1984) have suggested that orchid pollination system have evolved in response to competition for pollinators. Bose & Yadav (1986) has suggested that flower initiation in orchid is determined by the genotype, and its development is in interaction with the environmental conditions.

In Indian orchids very few literatures are available (Hegde, 1980; Joy, 1992; Wadhwa *et al.*, 1994). More emphasis has been paid to orchid growth and reproduction from phylogenetic and ecological point of view. Primack *et al.* (1994) studied the cause of reproduction, Allison Dennis (1989) studied the cost of flower and fruit production. Ackerman (1986, 1990) have also reported that orchid generally produce fewer fruits than flowers. The structural aspects of reproduction in some orchid species is also available *i.e.*, orchid fruit development is characterised by long periods necessary for mature embryo sac to form after pollination (Maheshwari, 1950; Writh & Withner, 1959; Veyret, 1974). The hormonal and structural aspect of fruit development in *Epidendrum* was reported by Dalyer *et al.* (1982). Differential fruit set on the inflorescence has been observed for several orchid species (Nelson, 1983, 1984; Cole & Firmage, 1984; Berry & Calvo 1991).

Perusal of the above cited literatures reveal that detailed phenological study is lacking in orchids.

**Palynology**: In angiosperms, morphological characters of pollen grains have been widely used in consideration of taxonomy and inter–relationship of plants at various taxonomic levels (Erdtmen, 1952; Woodhouse, 1935; Nair, 1965, 1985, 1991). Realizing its importance, many contributions has been made on the morphology of pollens in different plant groups (Drugg, 1962; Nowicke, & Miller, 1989; Constance & Chuang, 1982; Harley, 1986a,b; Patel *et al.*, 1985; Modgil, 1996; etc.). Exine architecture model for viscin threads and theory on the evolution of exine in orchidaceae was also put forward by Burns–Balogh (1983) and Hesse (1986) respectively.

As early as 1810, Brown recognised five sections in the family orchidaceae based upon pollen packing and texture. While Lindley (1826) based his section and tribes mainly upon pollinium characters. Recent studies seeking phylogenetic patterns within the family have employed all the pollen characters (Burns–Balogh & Funk, 1986; Dressler, 1990a,b,c, 1993).

A considerable number of studies on the palynology of the orchids are available in the literatures (Williams & Broome, 1976; Schill & Pfieffer, 1977; Ackerman & Williams, 1980, 1981; Balogh, 1979, 1982; Burns–Balogh, 1983; Hesse & Burns–Balogh, 1984; Newton & Williams, 1978; Fruedenstein & Rasmussen, 1996).

In Indian orchids few works has emerged in the recent years ( Chardard, 1971; Vij & Kashyap, 1978; Arora, 1985; Arora & Kapil, 1989; Joy *et al.* 1994). According to

Manilal & Kumar (1986), no comprehensive work has been done so far on the palynology of Indian orchids.

Reichenbach (1852) may have been the first to examine development of orchid pollen and associated structures. His survey of the pollen of 14 species has made many workers to infer that pollen morphology and organisation may be quite useful at higher taxonomic categories. Consequently, Williams & Broome (1976) reported that among the orchidaceae, the Epidendroids exhibit a wide range of diversity of pollen types. Williams (1970) has emphasised the importance of pollinaria and pollinia in the classification of Oncidinae. Arora (1985) suggested that the feature of pollinia, their shape, size and number can be employed at the specific level in the classification of *Dendrobium*. Ackerman & Williams (1981) also examined the pollen organisation of Chlorocinae and reported that it may be quite useful at higher taxonomic categories. Balogh (1979) opines that many species could be identified by characters like arrangement of tetrads in the pollinium, size and shape of tetrads, structure of exine etc.

The diversity in the nature and number of apertures has been one of the widely employed pollen characters for systematic and phylogenetic studies (Arora & Kapil, 1989). In 1990, they conducted studies on many Indian orchid species with respect to pollen organisation, sculpturing of the exine, pollen aperatures etc, and suggested further exploration on the large number of uninvestigated tropical and temperate orchids.

**Seed Morphometry**: Seed morphology serves a relatively common source of systematic characters to circumscribe sub generic groups or hypothesise relationship among species within a genus (Mathews & Levins, 1986; Ness, 1989). Investigators like Thieret (1955); Elisens (1985), Elisons & Tomb (1983), Takahashi, (1993) have used seed morphology to hypothesise relationship among genera. Beer (1863) have also numerous photographs and drawings on orchid seeds. A good number of recent papers are available on seed morphology of different plant species (Harper *et al.*, 1970; Krach, 1977; Hufford, 1988; Hidcki, 1993; Takahashi, 1993; Larry, 1995).

Characters associated with the orchid seed coat has been noted by Clifford & Smith (1969), Arditti *et al.* (1979, 1980), Healy *et al.* (1980), Barthlott & Ziegler (1981), Ziegler (1981) Tohda (1983, 1985, 1986), Chase & Pippen (1988, 1990), Molvray & Kores (1995). The systematic significance of overall seed shape, colour, size and their external–internal structure has been emphasised by Barthlott (1984).

Till date, the most comprehensive work on orchid seed morphology has been provided by Ziegler (1981), whose aspects were published in a short article by Barthlott & Ziegler (1981). Their survey of the family recognises 20 different seed types based on overall seed shape, and seed surface morphology.

Phylogenetic relationship within the orchidaceae has been discussed extensively in a series of recent papers (Garay, 1960, 1972; Dressler, 1981, 1986, 1990a,b,c, 1993; Rasmussen, 1982, 1986; Burns–Balogh & Funk, 1986). This has greatly increased our knowledge, but they are marked by controversy surrounding the delimitation of major lineages within the family. In order to compensate this lack of consensus on phylogenetic relationship, there has been other aspect like seed morphology provided by Barthlott (1976), Ziegler (1981), Chase & Pippen (1990), Chase & Hills (1992), Molvray & Kores (1995).

Patrick *et al.* (1980) suggested that morphometric analysis of orchid seeds indicate that testa and embryo dimensions, colour, presence or absence of reticulations on seed coat are of diagonistic value. The importance of scanning electron microscope studies on fine structure, general morphology and size of orchid seeds was emphasised by Arditti *et al.* (1979, 1980), Senghas *et al.* (1974), Barthlott (1976). Studies on orchid seed characters can solve not only taxonomic and phylogenetic problems, but it can also explain certain aspects on the orchid seed biology (Barthlott, 1976; Arditti *et al.*, 1979; Patrick *et al.*, 1980).

Perusal of literature reveals that only few studies on orchid seed morphology are available on Indian orchids Joy *et al.* (1994). Therefore this field of study is yet to be ventured and this would contribute greatly in solving taxonomic problems of *Vanda* group.

**Cytology**: The chromosome number determination and analysis of karyotypes of plants has now become imperative not only to show relationship between various categories of taxa but also in programmes involving breeding. Levan *et al.* (1964) has adopted a comprehensive chromosome classification and the methodology for chromosomal studies was also dealt in detail by him as well as Battaglia (1957a,b). However, orchids are generally recognised as difficult material so the staining technique standardised by Kamemoto *et al* (1966) is widely followed in orchid cytology.

The importance of cytology in clarifying taxonomy and evolution of orchid species has been established by various workers like Kamemoto (1961), Shindo & Kamemoto (1963), Sharma & Chatterji (1966, 1986, 1990), Sau & Sharma (1983).

According to Vij & Sood (1986), chromosome morphology of Indian orchids have been studied in more than 510 species. These data are mostly found to be accumulated from the northeastern Himalayas and southern India (Chatterji, 1966; Sharma & Chatterji, 1966; Mehra & Vij, 1970; Arora, 1971; Vij *et al.* 1976b; Mehra & Sehgal, 1980; Abraham & Vatsala, 1981; Sau & Sharma, 1983; Vij *et al.* 1983; Shekar, 1984; Mehra & Kashyap, 1984d; Hegde & Ingalhalli, 1985; Biswas, 1986; Freudenstein, 1984; Joy 1996).

The sub–tribe Sarcanthinae which also included *Vanda* group is taxonomically complex and therefore several authors have tried to trace genome homologies and phylogenetic affinities using chromosomal features (Tanaka & Kamemoto, 1961; Shindo & Kamemoto, 1963b; Sharma & Chatterji, 1966; Arends, 1970; Tara & Kamemoto, 1970; Roy & Sharma, 1972). These studies have shown a numerical stability of chromosomes 2n=38. However, occasional deviation from the normal run is also reported by Chardard (1963), Sharma & Chatterji (11966). Some *Vanda* species and hybrids have also been worked out by Woodard (1952), Storey (1952) and Storey *et al.* (1963). Despite the availability of literatures relating to cytodata on orchids, a thoroughly investigated chromosome number along with karyotype analysis is still lacking for a complete taxon.

# Chapter 3
# Biodiversity

Biological diversity, or 'biodiversity' is the total variability within all living organisms and the ecological complexes they inhabit. The concept of biological diversity is defined as the variety of life forms in a given region, the ecological roles they perform and the genetic diversity they contain (Wilcox, 1984). Though a variety of definitions and interpretations is provided in literature, a more comprehensive definition of biodiversity is provided by Reid and Miller (1989). According to them, "biodiversity is the variety of the world's organisms, including their genetic diversity and assemblages they form." A region with several individual species is said to be biologically diverse. Biological diversity can be measured at any level from global diversity to ecosystem, community, species, populations, individuals or even to genes within a single individual. Sepcies with several inter population differences, where each population gets genetically adapted to specific environmental conditions is said to be genetically diverse, *i.e.* genetic diversity of a species. From a biological perspective, generally three main subsystems are considered in the approach of biodiversity, viz., genetic, species and ecosystem diversity.

According to Waytt (1982), the orchideceae is an "individualist" family with "intensive genetic exploration". In orchids the extreme degree of morphological variability is attributed to genetic drift (Brieger, 1975). Genetic diversity often evolves because of interactions between different individuals of the same species and somtimes to other subsystem species. As species are the repositories of genetic diversity, species diversity is the most important aspect of biodiversity. The term biodivesity is generally used as a synonym of species biodiversity or species richness. Thus, species are the central objects to the concept of biodiversity and the knowledge of species taxonomy is the current currency of biodiversity (Heywood, 1996).

Today the concept of sustainable development becomes the most focused objective for the conservation of germplasm. In other words, the whole ranges of variation present within a particular species to maintain the potential for continuing evolution or genetic improvement for sustained supply of materials to human development and progress. Hence, biodiversity and taxonomic accounts are the primary steps in this management regime.

The genus *Vanda Jones* ex. R.Br. has great horticultural importance with fast growing demands in the orchid trade. In the last three decades, many hybrids have been produced which supersede other genera of the cultivated orchids. *Vandas* are grown commercially on a large scale in Thailand, Malaysia, Singapore, Hawaii and Southern Florida. Since India houses several *Vanda* species, a great potential exists to develop novel hybrids to fulfill the increasing demands in the international and domestic markets.

The *Vanda* group is an Indo–Malayan genus extending from India to South–east Asia, Borneo, Indonesia, Papua, New Guinea and North Australia with about forty species. The *Vanda* is a complicated and difficult genus in need of a taxonomic revision and more specimen to study (Christensen 1992). There are several attempts to suggest their affinities, segregation, and merger of the genera, and transfer of species. A new genus *Paplionanthe* was proposed by Schlechter (1926), Holttum (1959) for the terete–leaved *Vanda*. This separation of terete–leaved taxa from strap–leaved *Vanda* has been supported by authors like Tanaka & Kamemoto (1961) and Shindo & Kamemoto (1963a). Recently, Garay (1986) proposed *Trudelia* to include three species; viz., *T.alpina* (Lindl.) Garay, an Indian species *V.alpina* Lindl. *T.griffithi* (Lindl.) Garay and *T.chlorosanthe* Garay. Christenson (1992) proposed *Taprobanea* Christ. to include *V.spathulata*(L.) Spreng.

In India, the *Vanda* groups are found mostly scattered in the hilly states of the North–Eastern region including the Darjeeling district of West Bengal and few species are found in Uttar Pradesh, Madhya Pradesh, Orissa, Gujrat and the Western Ghats. The phytogeographical distribution is illustrated in Map–3.1. General account and occurrence of Indian *Vanda* have been documented right from the old literatures on Indian orchids, viz., Linnaeus "Species Plantarum" (1753); Brown (1821–22); Roxburgh's 'Flora Indica' (1832); Hooker (1895); King and Pantling (1898). So far, many recnet fragmentary literatures are available on this taxon by various workers of which a few important ones are – 11 species by Pradhan (1979), list of 9 species by Jain & Mehrotra (1984), 10 species by Karthikeyan *et al* (1989), but a comprehensive study is skill lacking. Therefore, a thorough survey on biodiversity of Indian *Vanda*, which is essential for correct scientific approach is taken up in this chapter.

## Generic Description:

***Vanda R. Br.***, Bot. Reg. t. 506. 1820; Endl. Gen. Pl.204. 1837; Benth. & Hook. f. Gen. Pl.3:578. 1883; Pfitz. in Engl. & Prantl. Pflanzenf. 2 (6): 214. 1889; Hook.f. Fl. Brit. Ind.6:49.1890; King & Pantl. Ann. Roy. Bot. Gard. Cal. 8:214. 1898; J.J. Smith, Fl. Buitenz. 6:590, 1905; Holtt. Fl. Malaya 1:713. cd. 2 1957; Holtt. Rev. Fl. Malaya 1:709. 1964; Seidenf. Orch. Gen. Thai. XIV. Op. Bot. 95:149. 1988; Seidenf. Op. Bot. 413. 1992.

**Type**: *V. tessellata* (Roxb.) W.J. Hook. ex G.Don.

The generic name *Vanda* W. Jones ex R. Br. is derived from the Sanskrit name used for an orchid species in Bengal. Th plant is known as *V. tessellata* (= *V. roxburghii*). Originally Sir William Jones (1795) used this name without specific epithet. However, Brown, R. (1820) validly published the generic account referring to Jones work.

*Vandas* are monopodial epiphytic orchids with stout stem and thick roots (Vermiform); stem short or long, usually erect covered with old leaf sheaths; leaves

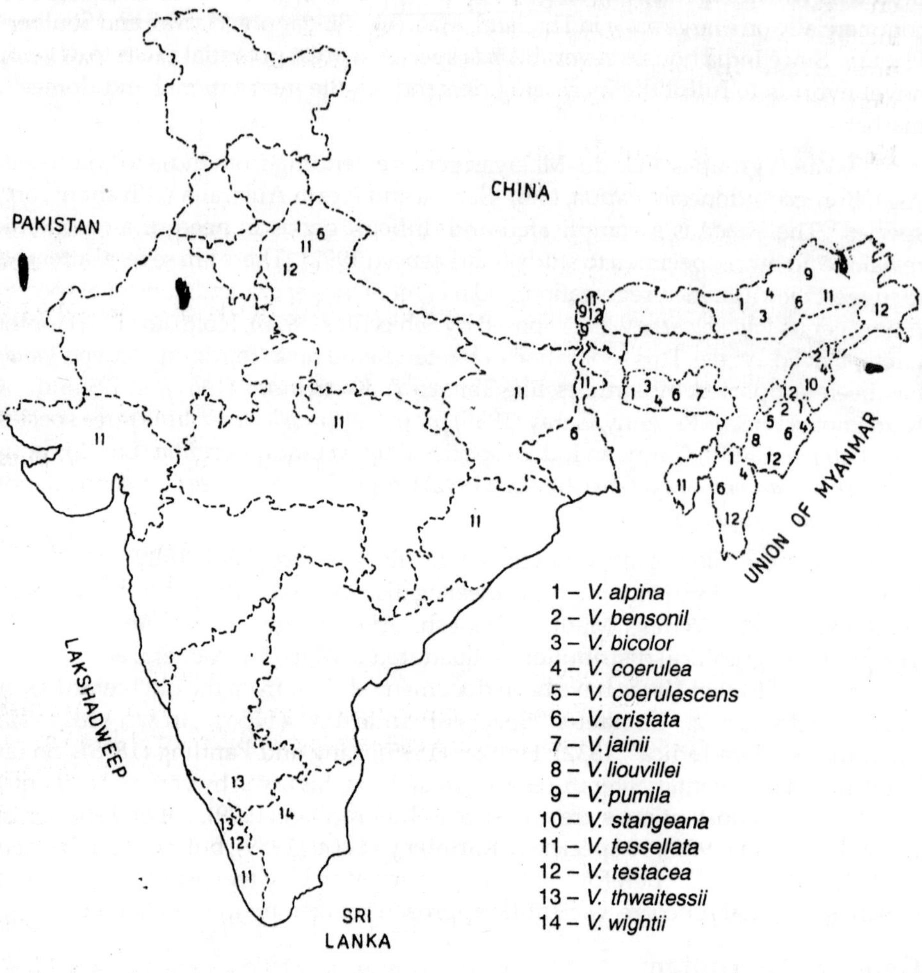


**Map 3.1: Distribution of Indian *Vanda* Species**

distichous/coriaceous, fleshy, keeled, apex obliquely 2–lobed, rarely acute, strap–shaped: Inflorenscence raceme, axillary, shorter or longer than leaves, more or less erect, few to many flowered : Flowers usually showy and lasting for several days, sepals and petals sub–equally spreading or twisted; narrowed to the base; often tessellated : Lip 3–lobed large, base saccate or spurred, attached immovably to the short column or foot, side lobes obscure or large; mid lobe fleshy, entire or lobed; disk lammellate; column short, stout: Anther 2–celled; Pollinia 2–cleft, ovoid, waxy, rostellum projection short, viscidium large, stipe short, one fertile anther.

The key for the identification of species, brief distinguishing characters of each species, their distrubution, endemism, extinction, notes on important observation and merger of species or their present taxonomic status are presented here. Details on vegetative and reproductive measurements of different organs or parts are also included for the ten *Vanda* species that has been collected and studied during the present investigation. All measurements were in centimeters. Length and breadth were measured along the longest and widest axis (Table 3.1 & 3.2).

## Key to the Species of Indian *Vandas*:

1a. Stem short, 15–25 cm long:

2a. Racemes 2–3 flowered; 2–2.5 cm across; sepals and petals greenish yellow; lip with a shallow sac, base rounded. .......................... ***V. alpina.***

2b. Racemes usually 1–3 flowered; flowers 2–2.5 cm across, sepals and petals pale yellowish or white:

3a. Sepals and petals yellow, lip with 2 horns. .............. ***V. cristata (= V. jainii).***

3b. Sepals and petals creamy white, lip with conical sac. ..... ***V. pumila.***

1b. Stem tall, 25–90 cm long:

4a. Inflorescence shorter than leaves or as long as leaves erect or sub–erect, usually 4–8 flowered:

5a. Flowers 3.5–4 cm across, yellowish.

6a. Lobules of lip squarish or 'fish–tail' shaped.

7a. Flowers 4 cm across, sepals and petals greenish to yellowish brown tessellated with reddish brown. ................................ ***V. stangeana.***

7b. Flowers 3.5–4.5 cm across, sepals and petals greenish to yellowish brown tessellated with brown. .. ***V. liouvillei.***

8a. Inflorescence 4–8 flowered; flowers 3–5 cm across, yellowish green with blue tinge. ........... ***V. tessellata.***

8b. Inflorescence up to 12 flowered; flowers 1.5–2 cm across yellow. ........................................... ***V. testacea.***

6b. Side lobes of lip subquadrate. ................................ ***V. wightii.***

5b. Flowers 5 cm or less than 5 cm across, brownish purple, obscurely tessellated. .................................................................. ***V. bicolor.***

4b. Inflorescence erect, many flowered longer than leaves:

9a. Flowers 12–14, 4–5 cm across, sepals and petals yellowish green. ................................... ***V. bensonii.***

9b. Flowers up to 20 or more; blue:

10a. Flowers 8–10 cm across, initially pale blue gradually becomes dark blue, flowering in autumn. .... ***V. coerulea.***

10b. Flowers 2–2.5 cm across, pale blue, flowering in summer. ........................... ***V. coerulescens.***

**Table - 3.1: Vegetative and inflorescence observation**

| Species | Stem | | Leaf | | | | | Inflorescence | | | | Floral bract | | | | No. of flowers |
|---|---|---|---|---|---|---|---|---|---|---|---|---|---|---|---|---|
| | nature | height (cm) | shape | L (cm) | B (cm) | L/B | apex | type | position | nature | L (cm) | shape | L (cm) | B (cm) | L/B | |
| *V. alpina* | woody | 25 | narrowly | 13.5 | 1.2 | 11.3 | unequally | raceme | axillary | sub-erect | 2.8 | ovate- | 0.4 | 0.5 | 0.8 | 2-3 |
| *V. bicolor* | woody | 40 | strap-like | 16.5 | 1.6 | 10.3 | unequally | raceme | axillary | sub-erect | 12.5 | ovate | 0.5 | 0.5 | 1.0 | 4-8 |
| *V. coerulea* | woody | 90 | strap-like | 20.0 | 2.5 | 8.0 | unequally | raceme | axillary | erect | 48.7 | ovate | 1.0 | 1.0 | 1.0 | 10-20 |
| *V. coerulescens* | woody | 25 | linear oblong | 16.0 | 1.5 | 10.7 | unequally | raceme | axillary | erect | 18.4 | ovate | 0.3 | 0.3 | 1.0 | 18-22 |
| *V. cristata* | woody | 22 | narrowly | 12.2 | 1.4 | 8.3 | unequally | raceme | axillary | sub-erect | 3.2 | ovate | 0.5 | 0.5 | 1.0 | 2-4 |
| *V. liouvillei* | woody | 45 | strap-like | 20.0 | 1.8 | 11.1 | unequally | raceme | axillary | sub-erect | 20.3 | ovate | 0.4 | 0.4 | 1.0 | 4-8 |
| *V. pumila* | woody | 15 | narrowly | 16.5 | 1.3 | 12.7 | unequally | raceme | axillary | sub-erect | 2.5 | ovate | 0.4 | 0.4 | 1.0 | 1-2 |
| *V. stangeana* | woody | 43 | strap-like | 21.0 | 1.8 | 11.7 | unequally | raceme | axillary | sub-erect | 22.0 | ovate | 0.4 | 0.4 | 1.0 | 4-8 |
| *V. tessellata* | woody | 40 | linear-oblong | 22.5 | 1.5 | 15.0 | unequally | raceme | axillary | erect | 14.5 | ovate | 0.4 | 0.4 | 1.0 | 4-8 |
| *V. testacea* | woody | 25 | linear-oblong | 16.4 | 1.3 | 12.6 | unequally | raceme | axillary | erect | 20.0 | ovate | 0.3 | 0.3 | 1.0 | 8-12 |

L = length; B = Breadth; L/B = length/breadth ratio

**Table 3.2 : Floral parts and seed pod measurements**

| Species | Pedicel Length (cm) | Ovary Length (cm) | Flower across (cm) | Dorsal sepal (cm) | | | Lateral sepal (cm) | | | Petal (cm) | | | Labellum (cm) | | | | Column length | Pollinia (cm) | | Seed pod length |
|---|---|---|---|---|---|---|---|---|---|---|---|---|---|---|---|---|---|---|---|---|
| | | | | L | B | L/B | L | B | L/B | L | B | L/B | L | B | L/B | Spur | | L | B | (cm) |
| *V. alpina* | 1.5 | 1.0 | 2.5 | 1.6 | 0.6 | 2.7 | 1.6 | 0.7 | 2.2 | 1.6 | 0.5 | 3.2 | 1.6 | 1.0 | 1.6 | 0.4 | 0.4 | 0 | 0.3 | 4.5 |
| *V. bicolor* | 2.8 | 1.4 | 4.5 | 2.5 | 1.3 | 1.9 | 2.5 | 1.7 | 1.4 | 2.2 | 1.5 | 1.4 | 2 | 1.0 | 2.0 | 06 | 0.6 | 0 | 0.3 | 5.6 |
| *V. coerulea* | 3.0 | 2.0 | 8.5 | 3.8 | 2.0 | 1.9 | 4.3 | 2.5 | 1.7 | 4.0 | 2.2 | 1.8 | 1.8 | 0.6 | 3.0 | 1.0 | 0.6 | 0 | 0.3 | 6.5 |
| *V. coerulescens* | 2.2 | 1.0 | 2.5 | 1.1 | 0.6 | 1.8 | 1.1 | 0.7 | 1.5 | 1.1 | 0.5 | 2.2 | 0.9 | 0.6 | 1.5 | 0.5 | 0.6 | 0 | 0.2 | 4.2 |
| *V. cristata* | 2.4 | 1.3 | 4.5 | 2.5 | 0.9 | 2.7 | 2.5 | 0.6 | 4.1 | 2.5 | 0.6 | 4.1 | 2.4 | 1.2 | 2.0 | 0.4 | 0.6 | 0 | 0.3 | 4.5 |
| *V. liouvillei* | 4.3 | 1.2 | 3.8 | 1.7 | 1.1 | 1.5 | 1.8 | 1.3 | 1.3 | 1.7 | 1.1 | 1.5 | 3.0 | 0.9 | 3.3 | 0.7 | 0.7 | 0 | 0.3 | 5.4 |
| *V. pumila* | 2.3 | 1.3 | 2.8 | 2.5 | 0.6 | 4.1 | 2.5 | 0.6 | 4.1 | 2.5 | 0.5 | 5.0 | 1.4 | 0.8 | 1.7 | 0.4 | 0.6 | 0 | 0.3 | - |
| *V. stangeana* | 4.0 | 1.5 | 3.5 | 1.7 | 1.1 | 1.5 | 1.8 | 1.5 | 1.2 | 1.8 | 1.1 | 1.6 | 2.5 | 1.1 | 2.2 | 0.5 | 0.7 | 0.1 | 0.3 | 5.0 |
| *V. tessellatea* | 3.0 | 1.5 | 4.5 | 2.7 | 1.4 | 1.9 | 2.7 | 1.7 | 1.5 | 2.3 | 1.4 | 1.6 | 1.8 | 1.2 | 1.5 | 0.8 | 0.6 | 0 | 0.3 | 7.5 |
| *V. testacea* | 1.3 | 1.2 | 1.8 | 0.8 | 0.5 | 1.6 | 0.8 | 0.5 | 1.6 | 0.8 | 0.4 | 2.0 | 1.2 | 0.4 | 3.0 | 0.3 | 0.2 | 0 | 0.2 | 3.7 |

L = length; B = Breadth; L/B = length/breadth ratio

***Vanda alpina*** Lindl., Fl. Orch. *Vanda* 10. 1853; Hook. f. Fl. Brit. Ind. 6:53. 1890; King & Pantl. Ann. Roy. Bot. Gard. Cal. 8:217. t. 289. 1898; Duthie, Ann. Roy. Bot. Gard. Cal. 9 (2): 164. 1906; et Cat. Pl. Kumaun 178. 1906; Hara *et al.*, Enum. Fl. Pl. Nep. 57. 1978; Pradhan, Indl. Orch. II:569. 1979; Banerji & Pradhan, Orch. Nep. Him. 516. t. 243. 1984; Hegde, Orch. Ar.P. 82. 1984; Jain & Mehrotra, Pril. Inv. Orch. Ind. 127. 1984; Kataki, Orch. Megh. 176. 1984; Deva & Naith. Orch. Fl. N. W. Him. 435. t. 453. 1986; Karthikeyan *et al.*, Fl. Ind. Enu. Monocot. 175. 1989; Pangtey *et al.*, Orch. Kumaun Him. 174. 1991. *Luisia alpina* Lindl. in Bot. Reg. Misc. 56:1858.

Plant grows up to 25 cm with leaves narrowly oblong, conduplicate and unequally bilobed at the apex. Inflorescence semi erect and very short bearing 2–3 flowers. Flowers are always found to be nodding. Sepals and petals narrowly oblong, yellowish–green in colour. Lip adnate to the column, 3–lobed, side lobe shallow rounded, mid lobe ovate concave with tip bifid; ground lip is pale yellow with dark purple streaks.

**Flowering Season:** July – August.

**Distribution:** India, (U.P. Hills, Arunachal Pradesh, Manipur, Meghalaya, Mizoram & Nagaland), Nepal & Bhutan.

**Specimens Examined:** Meghalaya, Mawlai, *Limasenla* 17031(NEHU); Upper shillong, 17010 (NEHU); Jarain–Jaintia hills, *Y.Kumar* 17002 (NEHU).

**Note:** Good for breeding as plants are small with long lasting flowers. Recently Garay (1986) has proposed a new genus for *V alpina* Lindl. under *Trudelia* Garay. However, a separate genus *Trudelia* cannot be accepted basing on ringent floral segments and the spur length. Morever, other species included in *Trudelia* have spreading floral segments. Present investigaions have affirmed to retain it under *Vanda* only. An interesting population with deeper shades of streaks in the lip (Plate – 3.1b) has been discovered from Meghalaya.

***Vanda bensonii*** Batemen, ex Hook. f. in Bot. Mag. 92. t. 5611. 1866; Reichb. f. in Gard. Chron. 1867. 180. Fig; in Xen. Orch. 2:138. 1868; 136.1874; Parish, 175. 198. 1883; Hook. f. Fl. Brit. Ind. 6:57. 1890; Grant, Orch. Urma, 247. 1895; Seidenf & Smitnd. Orch. Thai. 4(1):579. t. 433. 1963; Kam. & Sagk. 73. 1975; S.Y.Hu in Quart. Journ. Taiwan. Mus. 28:381.1975; Winkler, 1978.

Stem short, leaf apex with one long obtuse lobule, half obliquely praemorsely cut off. Inflorescence erect bearing many flowers. Sepals and petals yellowish green usually not distantly tessellated but with many dark red sports often in rows along the veins, lip equally long as the sepals, rosy purple with white spur.

**Flowering Season:** March – April

**Distribution:** India (Manipur & Nagaland), Myanmar.

**Specimens Examined:** Not collected.

**Note:** It is allied to *V. stangeana* and grows with it in nature. Reported by

Seidenfaden (1982) and Mukherjee (1983), from Manipur Bordering Myanmar. Despite a number of endeavours to locate this species from the reported habitats, the venture has yet been unsuccessful. Hence this species is rare with limited distribution and seems to be extinct in nature.

***Vanda bicolor*** Griff. Notul. 3:354. 1851; Reichb. f. in Gard. Chron. 650, 1875; Hook. f. Fl. Brit. Ind. 6:52. 1890; Jain & Mehrotra, Pril. Inv. Orch. Ind. 127. 1984; Karthikeyan *et al.*, Fl. Ind. Enu. Monocot. 175. 1989.

Stem grows up to 40 cm with recurved leaves, unequally bilobed at the apex. Inflorescence sub erect with 4–8 flowers. Sepals and petals obovate obtuse spathulate, greenish–brown obscurely tessellated with dark brown, tip of the lip contracted, side lobe orbicular, mid lobe small and panduriform, 2 lobed purple in colour. It can be easily distinugished by the large orbicular side lobes.

**Flowering Season:** March – April.

**Distribution:** India (Arunachal Pradesh & Meghalaya) and BHUTAN.

**Specimens Examined:** Arunchal Pradesh, Zero, *Limasenla* 17013 (NEHU); Meghalaya, Tura, West Garo Hills, *Y.Kumar* 17005 (NEHU).

**Note:** It is allied to *V. tessellata* but differs by their large orbicular side lobes of the lip. This plant has been collected from Arunachal Pradesh though Hegde (1984) did not include this species in his account. This is one of the lesser known *Vanda* species.

***Vanda coerulea*** Griff., ex. Lindl., in Bot. Reg. 1847; Lindl. Fol. Orch. *Vanda* 18.1853; Reichb. f. Xen. Orch. 1:8. t. 5. 1854; Clarke, 73. 1889; Hook. f. Fl. Brit. Indl. 6:51, 1890; Seidenf & Smitnd. Orch. Thai. 4(1):577. 1963; Holtt. Fl. Malaya 1:722. 1967; Kam & Sagk. 72. 1975; Pradhan, Indl. Orch. II:567. 1979; Bechtel *et al.*, Man. Cult. Orch. Sp. 410. 1981; Hegde, Orch. Ar. P. 82. 1984; Jain & Mehrotra, Pril. Inv. Orch. Ind. 127. 1984; Kataki, Orch. Megh. 174. 1984; Cheng & Tang, 216. 1986; Seidenf. Op. Bot. 95:196. 1988; Karthikeyan *et al.*, Fl. Ind. Enu. Monocot. 175. 1989; *Vanda* sp. Griff. Itin. Not. 88. no.1284.1848.

This species is one of the most outstanding Indian *Vanda*. The plant grows up to 90 cm tall with strap shaped oblong leaves. A well grown single inflorescence bears more than 20 flowers. Flowers elegantly tessellated, two lateral petals are twisted to about 180°; lip is deeper blue and much shorter than the sepals, 3–lobed, side lobe small and rounded, mid lobe oblong, tip contracted, bifid and dark blue.

**Flowering Season:** September – Novemeber.

**Distribution:** India (Manipur, Meghalaya, Mizoram & Nagaland) Myanmar and Thailand.

**Specimens Examined:** Nagaland, Mokokochung, *Limasenla* 17017 (NEHU); Meghalaya, Khasi Hills, Ri–Bhoi area, *Y. Kumar* 17015 (NEHU); Jaintia hills, Jarain, *Y. Kumar* 17014 (NEHU).

**Note:** Few orchids surpass the beauty of blue *Vanda* flowers. This species is still in great demand for its breeding qualities, viz., wide range of adaptability from tropical to sub tropical climate. A considerable variaton in size and colour of floral segments is observed in nature (Plate – 3.1d).

***Vanda coerulescens*** Griff., Not. 3:352, Ic. t. 331. 1851; Reichb. f. in Walp. Ann. 6:868/ 1864; Hook. f. Fl. Brit. Ind. 6:50. 1890; Grant, Orch. Burma, 249. 1895; Hossseus, 382. 19111; Holtt. Fl. Malaya. 722. 1957; Seidenf. & Smitnd. Orch. Thai. 4(1):583. 1963; Kam & Sagk. 73.1975; Pradhan. Int. Orch. II:567. 1979; Bechtel *et al.*, Man. Cult. Orch. Sp. 411. 1981; Hegde, Orch. Ar. P. 83. 1984; Cheng & Tang, Acta. Bot. Yun. VIII.2.217. 1986; Seidenf. Orch. Gen. Thai. XIV. Op. Bot. 95:208. 1988.

The plant is similar to *V. testacea* although the leaves are much thicker and broader. Inflorescence grows up to 18 cm bearing more than 20 flowers. Sepals and petals oblong spathulate, light blue without tessellation. Lip rather shorter than the sepals, side lobe small acute, mid lobe obovate. tip truncate, 2–lobed dark blue, spur slender.

**Floweing Season:** June

**Distribution:** India (Manipur), Myanmar, China and Thailand.

**Specimens Examined:** Manipur, Churachandpur, *Limasenla* 71032 (NEHU); Ukhrul, *Y. Kumar* 17055 (NEHU).

**Note:** Sometimes the species is confused with *V. coerulea* but it can be distinguisehd by its smaller size and light coloured flowers. Two varieties *boxalii* Reichb. f. and *lowiana* Reichb. f. are known to occur. This is one of the best miniature *Vanda* species to be used for breeding and improvement.

***Vanda cristata*** Lindl., Gen. & Sp. Orch. 216. 1833; Hook. f. Fl. Brit. Ind. 6:53. 1893; King & Pantl. Ann. Roy. Bot. Gard. Cal. 8:216. t. 287. 1898; Duthie, Ann. Roy. Bot. Gard. Cal: 9(2):146. 1906; et. cat. Pl. Kumaun 178. 1906; Hara *et al.*, Emu. Fl. Pl. Nep. 57. 1978; Pradhan, Ind. Orch. II:570. 1979; Banerji & Pradhan, Orch. Nep. Him. 518. t. 244. 1984; Hegde,Orch. Ar. P. 83. 1984; Jain & Mehrotra, Pril. Inv. Orch. 128. 1984; Kataki, Orch.Megh. 175. 1984: Deva & Nath. Orch. Fl. N. W. Him. 439. t. 254. 1986; Karthikeyan *et al.*, Fl. Ind. Enu. Monocot. 175. 1989; Pangtey *et al.*, Orch. Kumaun Him.174. 1991; *Aerides cristatum* wall. mss. Aerides sp. Griff. Itin. Notes. 203. No. 1188.

The plant is miniature with narrow oblong leaves. A single plant may bear usually 3 spikes with 1–3 flowers in each. Sepals and petals oblong lanceolate and yellowish green. Side lobe of the lip triangular acute, mid lobe oblong concave. Unlike any other *Vanda* species, apical portion of the lip possess two distinct horn like structures.

**Flowering Season:** March – April.

**Distribution:** India (U.P.Hills, Arunachal Pradesh, Manipur, Meghalaya, Mizoram & Nagaland), Nepal and Bhutan.

**Specimens Examined:** Meghalaya, Dawki–Jaintia hills, *Limasenla* 17004 (NEHU); Ri–Bhoi area *Limasenla* 17016 (NEHU); Umtingar (Jaintia hills), *Y. Kumar* 17020 (NEHU).

**Note:** Flowers remain fresh for a month which is favoured by the hobbyists. *V. cristata var. multiflora* Hort. is also repotred from Darjeeling and Sikkim where the flower size is smaller and it may bear up to 5 in each spike. A variation in the colour of the lip has also been observed in the experimental net house (Plate – 3.2b).

*Vanda jainii* Chauhan in J. Econ. Tax. Bot., 5(5):977–79, 1984.

Stem grows upto 20–24 cm tall, leaves narrowly oblong, keeled, equally trilobed, mucrnate at tip. Racemes 2.1–2.4 cm long, 2–flowered. Shorter than leaves. Flowers 4.0 – 4.5 cm across, greenish yellow, lip with brown stripes. Bract ovate, acute. Sepals oblong obtuse yellowish, 7–paralleled nerved, lateral petal 5–paralleled nerved, shorter than sepals. Lip fleshy adnate to the column, shorter than lateral sepals, trilobed, spurred, side lobe broad erect, triangular. Apex with 2 erect lobules and a horn like fleshy, beak downwards, upper surface with 8–9 shallow smooth brown ridges and furrows (Chauhan, 1984).

**Flowering Season:** March – August.

**Distribution:** India (Meghalaya).

**Specimens Examined:** Meghalaya, Sonapur, Chauhan 70887 (Assam).

**Note:** Endemic to North–East India. Allied to *V. cristata* but differs by the leaf apex equally tri–lobed, lip shorter than the lateral sepal, apical lobes with two erect lobules at apex, upper surface of the lip with 8–9 smooth purple ridges and furrows, spur not distinct, saccate (Chauhan, 1984).

*Vanda liouvellei* Finet., in Not. Syst. (Paris) 2:299. t. 6. 1913; Seidenf. & Smitnd. Orch. Thai. 577. t. 432. Pl. 26. 1963; Kam. & Sagk. 171. t. 74. 1975; Kenn. Orch. Dig. 43:44. 1979; Seidenf. Orch. Gen. Thai. XIV. Op. Bot. 95: 204. t. 205. 1988; Seidenf. Op Bot.114:414. t. 415. 1992; Phukan, Orch. Rev. (104):189–90. 1996.

The plant is very similar to *V. stangeana* with channelled recurved leaves. Inflorescence sub erect bearing 4–8 flowers. Sepals and petals orbicular oblong, greenish to yellowish brown tessellated irregularly with deep brown. Lip white, side lobe triangular obtuse, midlobe obovate panduriform speckled with red, lip longer than the sepals and the tip is broadly bilobulate, fish–tail which turns brown in colour.

**Flowering Season:** April – May.

**Distribution:** India (Manipur), Myanmar.

**Specimens Examined:** Manipur, Ukhrul hills, *Limasenla* 17006 (NEHU)

**Note:** Not much has been mentioned in literature about this species. Originally collected from Myanmar, it was named after M. Liouville in whose collection the plant flowered in 1912. Seidenfaden (1988), Seidenfaden & Smitinand (1963 as *Vanda brunea*), Kamemoto & Sagarik (1975 as *Vanda* *brunea*), Kennedy (1979 as *Vanda bruenea*) and more recently Phukan (1995) has reported as a new record from India.

***Vanda pumila*** Hook. f., Fl. Brit. Ind. 6:53. 1890; King & Pantl. Ann. Roy. Bot. Gard. Cal. 8:216. t. 288. 1898; Guill, 394. 1955c; 273. 1959a; Seidenf. & Smitnd. Orch. Thai. 4(1); 583 1963; Batta. Bull. Bot. Soc. Beng. 23:163. 1969; Pradhan, Ind, Orch. II:570. 1979; Bechtel *et al.*, Man. Cult. Orch. Sp. 411. 1981; Seidenf. & Arora, 25. 1982; Jain & Mehrotra, Pril. Inv. Orch. 128. 1984; Kataki, Orch. Megh. 175. 1984; Seidenf. Orch. Gen. Thai. XIV. Op. Bot. 95:209. t. 131. 1988; Cheng & Tang. Acta. Bot. Yun. VIII.2. 217. 1986; Deva & Naith. Orch. Fl. N. W. Him. 439. t. 255. 1986; Karthikeyan *et al.*, Fl. Indl. Enu. Monocot. 175.1989; Pangtey *et al.*, Orch. Kumaun Him. 175. 1991; Seidenf. Orch. Indo. Op. Bot. 114:209. t. 285. 1992.

Stem up to 20 cm, leaves narrowly oblong, unequally bilobed at the apex. Inflorescence shorter than the leaves bearing 1–3 drooping flowers. Sepals and petals oblong obtuse, creamy white with sweet fragrance. Lip shorter than sepals, 3–lobed, side lobe rounded, streaked with purple, mid lobe broadly ovate concave, tip truncate retuse, spur with a conical sac.

**Flowering Season:** May – June.

**Distribution:** India (Arunachal Pradesh, Meghalaya, Sikkim & Darjeeling), Myanmar and Thailand.

**Specimens Examined:** Meghalaya, Nongstoin (W. Khasi hills), *Y. Kumar* 17022 (NEHU); Darjeeling, *Limasenla* 17025 (NEHU)

**Note:** Jain &Mehrotra (1984), and Pradhan (1979) reported this species as endemic to Eastern Himalays. However, it has been reported from Myanmar and Thialand, Seidenfaden (1982). But Grant (1895) does not include this species from Myanmar. This species is worth utilising for breeding due to its miniature habit and sweet scented flowers.

***V. stangeana*** Reichb. f., in Bot. Zeit. XIV (1858) 357; Hook.f. Fl. Brit. Ind.6:54. 1890; Pradhan, Ind. Orch. II:569. 1979; Bose and Batt. Orch. Ind. 518. 1980; Hegde.Orch. Ar. P. 83. 1984; Jain & Mehrotra, Pril. Inv. Orch. Ind. 128. 1984; Karthikeyan *et al.*, Fl. Ind. Enu. Monocot. 175. 1989.

Plant grows up to 45 cm with channeled recurred leaves unequally bilobed at the apex. Inflorescence with 4–8 flowers. Flowers resemble *V. liouvillei* but are distinguished by their permanent chestnut brown tessellation. Sepals and petals orbicular and clawed. Side lobe of the lip triangular obtuse, mid lobe obovate panduriform, white with streak of red dots, tip bifurcated and recurved.

**Flowering Season:** April – May

**Distribution:** India (Arunachal Pradesh, Manipur & Nagaland).

**Specimens Examined:** Nagaland, Mokokchung, *Limasenla* 17027 (NEHU); Manipur, Ukhrul hills, *Limasenla* 17006 (NEHU); Ukhrul, Senapati, *Y. Kumar* 17028 (NEHU).

Plate – 3.1: (a) *V. alpina*, (b) Variation, (c) *V. coerulea*, (d) Variation

Plate – 3.2: (a) *V. cristata*, (b) Variation, (c) *V. stangeana*, (d) Variation

Plate – 3.3: (a) *V. pumila*, (b) *V. coerulescens*, (c) *V. tessellata*, (d) Variation

Plate – 3.4: (a) *V. bicolor*, (b) *V. testacea*, (c) *V. liouvillei*, (d) *V. bensonii*

**Note:** This species is adaptable to a wide range of climates from sub tropical to tropical. It can be used in breeding for its straight and open displayed flower parts. Variation in colour at he tip of the lip (pale yellow) was observed (Plate –3.2d).

***V. tessellata*** (Roxb.) Hook. ex. G. Don, Lond. Hort. Brit. 372. 1830; Fischer & Gamble, Fl. Pres.Madras;1445(1910), 1928; Sant. & Kapad. Orch. Bomb. 220. 1966; Pradhan, Ind. Orch. II:569. 1979; Abrah. &Vat. Int. Orch. 438. t. 129. 1981; Banerji & Pradhan, Och. Nep. Him. 520. t. 245, 1984; Hegde, Orch. Ar. P. 82. 1984; Jain & Mehrotra, Pril. Inv. Orch. Ind. 128. 1984; Deva & Naith. Orch. Fl. N. W, Him. 439. t. 256. 1986; Karthikeyan *et al.*, Fl. Ind. Enu. Monocot. 175. 1989; Pangtey *et al.*, Orch. Kumaun Him. 176.1991; *Epidendrum tessellatum* Roxb., Pl. Chron.1:34. t. 42. 1795. *Vanda roxburghii* R. Br., Bot. 6. t. 506. 1820; Wt. Ic. t. 3(2):10. t. 916. 1844 – 45; Hook. f. Fl.Brit. Ind. 6:52. 1890; Duthie, Ann.roy. Bot. Gard. Cal. 9:145. 1906; Hara *et al.*, Enum. Fl. Pl. Nep. 58. 1978.

Plant grows up to 30 – 40 cm with recurved linear oblong leaves unequally bilobed at the apex. Inflorescence erect bearing 4–8 pendulous flowers. Sepals and petals orbicular oblong, slightly fleshy, scented. Lip white speckled with violet inside, side lobe small acute, midlobe obovate panduriform, tip contracted bifid, lilac blue or purple.

**Flowering Season:** April – June.

**Distribution:** India (U.P.Hills, Kishangang – Bihar, Siliguri – N.Bengal, Sikkim, Arunachal Pradesh, Tripura, Oriss, M.P., Gujarat, South India), Myanmar and Sri Lanka.

**Specimens Examined:** West Bengal, Siliguri, *Limasenla* 17012 (NEHU); way to Kalimpong 17021 (NEHU); Bihar Kishanganj, *Y. Kumar* 17020 (NEHU); Karnataka, Konkan, N. Konara, *Y. Kumar* 17026 (NEHU).

**Note:** It is intriguing that wide range of variations has been repoted. The *var. rufescens* have segments in varying shade of pink with pink lip is said to have bronze–pink root tips (Plate–3.3d) and *var. lutescens* have shades of yellow with lip colour ranging from pink through blue to white, bears clear yellow root tips. The species is extremely adaptable and lends itself to easy culture. The generic name *Vanda* originated for a Sanskrit word describing this plant species.

***Vanda testacea*** (Lindl.) Reichb. f., in Gard. Chron. 2. 166. 1877; Alston, 1931 : 277. t. 402. 1938; Fischer, 143. 1938; Sant. & Kapad. Orch. Bomb. 219–20. 1966; Kammathy *et al.*, 230. 1967; Sebastine & Vivek, 182. 1967; Rathakrishnan, 5. 1971; Abrah. & Vat. Int. Orch. 436. t.128, 1981; Ranghana *et al.*, 84. 1981; Raizada *et al.*, Orch. Mussoorie, 43. 1981; Joseph, 130. t. 112. 1983; Seidenf. & Arora, 25. 1982; Seidenf. 1599. 1983; Banerji & Pradhan, Orch. Nep. Him. 522. t. 246. 1984; Jain & Mehrotra, Pril. Inv. Orch. Ind. 1281984; Cheng & Tang, Acta. Bot. Yun. VIII.2. 217. 1986; Deva & Naith. Orch. Fl. N. W. Him. 411. 6. 257. 1986; Seidenf. Orch. Gen. Thai. XIV. Op. Bot. 95:208. 1988; Karthikeyan *et al.*, Fl. Ind. Enu. Monocot. 175. 1989; Pangtey *et al.*, Orch. Kumaun Him. 176. 1991. *Aerides testaceum* Lindl, Gen. Sp. Orch. 238. 1833.

*Arides wightiana* Lindl. cat. no. 7320. 1832 nom. nud; Gen. & Sp. Orch. 238. 1833; Wight, 8. 1852; Lidl. 40. 1859; Bot. Mag. t. 5138. 1859; Dalzeal & Gibson, 265. 1861; Thwaites, 305. 1864; Pradhan, Indl. Orch. II:567. 1979. *Vanda spathulata* auct. non (L.)Spreng; Graham, cat. Bomb. Pl. 204. 1839. *Vanda parviflora* Lindl., Bot Reg. 30: misc. 45. 1844; Wt. Ic. t. 1669. 1852; Hook. f. Fl. Brit. Ind. 6:50. 1890; King & Pantl. Ann. Roy. Bot. Gard. Cal. 8:215. t. 286. 1898; Duthie, Ann. Roy. Bot. Gard. Cal. 9:144. 1906; Fischer & Gamble, Fl. Pres. Madras : 1444 (1010).1928; Seidenf. & Smitnd. Orch. Thai. 584. 1963; Hara *et al.*, Enum. Fl. Pl. Him. 58. 1978.

The plant grows up to 10–20 cm. leaves fleshy, coriaceous, unequally bilobed. Inflorescence erect up to 20 cm long, with 8–20 flowers. Sepals and petals oblong obtuse, creamy yellow, widely spreading, side lobe obovate obtuse, mid lobe obovoid oblong, violet with two pappillate.

**Flowering Season:** May – June.

**Distribution:** India (H.P., U.P.Hills, Sikkim, Arunachal Pradesh, Manipur, Mizoram, Nagaland, through out Southern peninsular India in hilly tracts & Kerala), Myanmar, Thailand and Sri Lanka.

**Specimens Examined:** Karnataka, Dharwad, *Limasenla* 17008 (NEHU); Kerala, Pambhar, *Y. Kumar* 17029 (NEHU).

**Note:** Among the Indian *Vanda*s this species has the smallest flowers.

***Vanda wightii*** Reichb. f., in Walp. ann. 6:932. 1861; Hook. f. Fl. Brit. Ind. 6:54, 1890; Jain & Mehrotra, Pril. Inv. Orch. Ind. 128. 1984; Karthikeyan *et al.*, 176. 1989.

Leaves narrowly ligulate, unequally bilobed, lax–flowered, side lobes of lip subquadrate, midlobe broadly ovate, lip contracted, ligulate obtusely 2–lobed, disk with 2 thick ridges, spur conical, column slender.

**Flowering Season:** March – June.

**Distribution:** India (Nilgiri hills).

**Specimens Examined:** Not Collected.

**Note:** Endemic to Nilgiri hills, allied to *V. stangeana* Reichb. f. this species is supposed to be extinct as it has not been resighted in the wild ever since Wight's collection.

## Discussion

Present study reveals that, out of forty *Vanda* species which are mainly distributed in the Indo–Malayan region, India is a major natural habitat of *Vanda* with thirteen species. These are *V. alpina, V.bensonii, V.bicolor, V. coerulea, V. coerulescens, V. cristata, V.jainii, V.liouvillei, V.pumila, V.stangeana, V.tessellata, V.testacea* and *V. wightii*. Of these, *V. wightii* is no more existing in the recorded locality and could be considered as extinct.

The phytogeographical distribution of Indian *Vanda*s suggests that the North–Eastern region harbour maximum number of species. Orchid habitats are directly influnced by temperature, rainfall and altitude, besides microclimatic conditions.

Most probable reason for the occurrence of maximum number of species could be the humid forests in combination with various ecological and adaphic factors exclusive to North–East India. On the other hand, *V. tessellata* and *V.testacea* are moderately continuous in distribution extending from North to Southern India. According to Hegde (1985), number of species in a given region is almost inversely proportional to the distance from their migration. Based on phytogeographical distribution of Indian *Vanda* with maximum number and diversity of species in North–Eastern region it may be suggested that most species under study are Himalayan in origin or have migrated from neighbouring regions. Therefore, North–Eastern region including eastern Himalays and neighbouring regions could be considered as cradle of this taxon.

During the present study *V. bensonii* and *V. jainii* could not be located in nature despite several attempsts to do so. It is believed that *V. jainii* can only be some extreme variation of *V. cristata* or their population has reduced to a new extinction. *V. bensonii* also could not be located during the present investigation. Perhaps this species could be location specific or very rare. Several variatons are seen within the *Vanda* species observed in natural habitat and also in the experimental net house. The variations exibited within the species can be either due to environmental influence or the genetic make up of the species . Morever, the biodiversity within each species is the result of combined effects of the phylogenetic, geographical and ecological factors that are unique to each region. This leads to the idea that species richness and their variations certainly play an improtant role in prioritising the diversity centres.

However, the natural population are getting depleted due to over exploitation, habitat destruction, urbanisation, etc. Current resurgence of interest in species may also lead to further demand of species. Thus, breeding with a view to conserve these species is an important strategy. It is also anticipated that orchid enthusiasts would play immense attention to this outstanding group of orchids.

# Chapter 4
# Phenology

Phenology is "the art of observing life cycle phases or activity of plants and animals in their temporal occurrence throughout the year." (Leith, 1974). Plant phenology deals with the study of the seasonal patterns of leafing, flowering and fruiting in relation to the climate. This study has been a topic of scientific study since the 18th century (Aitken, 1974). It is of great interest in agriculture where the timing of flower and fruit production can be critical in determining crop yield. The concept and significance of phenological research lies in the fact that it constitutes a synthetic approach to evaluate plant response to the total environment. However, a close correlation exists between some phenological events and certain environmental factors which seem to serve as the master controlling factors (Jackson, 1966). Studies on phenological patterns of plants are important in germplasm collection and also for better understanding of the ecological adaptations of individual species and their interactions (Sten & Roachi, 1974; Waser, 1979; Thomson 1980). The periodicaty of different phenophases reflect availability of specific resources like flower, pollen/ pollinia, fruit and seeds during a particular period of a calender. Such informations are prerequisite for biodiversity conservation, their sustainable use and scientific multiplication programmes.

The phenology of flowering and fruiting is seasonally variable among species which is directly correlated to the total environmental response. Generally, phenological studies are based on observations of periodic phenomena occuring at a given location over a period of several years. Early workers are of the opinion that phenological events involving reproductive activity in plants are more closely correlated with temperature than other climatic factors. However, the microclimate merits attention in phenological study because it represents the actual conditions that influence plant response. Correlations should therefore be improved in a local study by sampling the microclimate of an area immediately affecting the phenological event.

Generally three environmental or phenological triggers have been identified, viz. photoperiod, temperature and moisture (Rathcke & Lacy, 1985; Loomis & Connor, 1992). These three factors can be regarded as the switches that break bud dormancy and start the devleopmental processes. Once set in motion these processes advanced as a function of temperature, day length, or a combination of the two. In orchids the sequence of flowering varies from species to species. This order reflects on the different phenological requirements which happen to be quite diverse. Therefore, using climate and flowering data, determination of the flowering triggers and the developmental requirements for each species can be evaluated.

Although a considerable emphasis has been paid to the study of orchid growth and their reproduction form phylogenetic and ecological point of view, few literatures are available on the phenology of Indian orchids in general. Phenological studies on Indian *Paphiopedilum* have been conducted by Joy (1996). However, there is no comprehensive work on Indian *Vandas*. In orchids, chronological events on reproductive phenophases indicates their seasonal response to flower bud initiation, flowering, fruit initiation, maturaltion and dehiscence which are important aspects for breeding and mass production of desired plants in the orchid trade. The objective of this study is to find out the periodicity (timing) of different phenophases and define precisely the calender of reproductive phenophaes on Indian species of *Vanda*.

## Materials and Methods

The phenological study for *Vanda* was carried out for all the species included in the present study. For the purpose, experimental plants were identified and collected from their natural habitats by giving the field numbers. For each species at least 10 plants were grown and maintained almost under natural conditions in the orchid net house at Botany Department, NEHU, Shillong. All the plants were given their respective accession numbers. The studies pertaining to phenological observation were made for three consecutive years from 1995 to 1997.

In this chapter, the chief emphasis has been focused ont he reproductive phenophases. Important events from the emergence of inflorescence primordia to seed pod dehiscence were recorded throughout the study period. The criteria used to access the phenological observation were : (a) emergence of the first and successive inflorescence primordia which wre marked simultaneously; (b) the number of days till the opening of the first flower i.e. anthesis period; (c) flowering season was considered practically from the first flower opening till the abscission of the last flower; (d) longevity of the individual flower; (e) seed pod initiation and, (f) browning and dehiscence was evaulated by daily observation of the marked plants. Emergence of inflorescence primordia, flowering season, browning and dehiscence of the seed pod were recorded in intervals of months. Anthesis period, longevity of individual flower and seed pod initiation were recorded in intervals of days.

## Climate of the study site

Climate data for the study period was obtained fromthe Seismological Department at Shillong. Monthly average readings for temperature, rainfall and relative humidity for the three consecutive years (1995, 1996 & 1997) were calculated on the basis of the daily recordings. From these three year data, their means for each corresponding month was calculated and represented graphically along with some phenological events.

## Results and Observations

### Climate observations

The climate of the study site, Shillong plateau, the capital of Meghalaya in the north-eastern region of India is situated in the rain shadow with an altitude of 1500 m and located at 25.6°N latitude and 91.90°E longitude. This climatic factors during this three year study period can be briefly summarised as follows - during summer, the maximum temperature ranged between 22°C and 26°C, and its lowest was 14°C in winter. The minimum temperature never rose above 19°C even in the summer while it remained below 14°C from October till next April dipping below 6°C in January. Heavy rainfall (above 350 mm) occurred from June to August, while from November to next March it was less (below 50 mm). The evening relative humidity (at 17:30) remained above 85% for most part of the year except from February to May. It was lower than 75% in March and April. The morning relative humidity (8:30) was found to be lower than 70% from October till next April. March was very dry in the mornings (58%). During summer the morning relative humidity steadily increased to above 85%. Relative humidity is alwasy higher in the evenings than in the mornings.

It is well estalished that photoperiod play an important role in plant life cycles. In the discussions, the day-lengths were roughly assumed according to the season of the year.

### Phenological observatios

The inter phenophase from the emergence of inflorescence primordia to dehiscence of the seed pod are discussed below (Table - 4.1). Simultaneouly, these events are also summarised basing on the climate data of temperature, rainfall and relative humidity (Figs. 4.1, 4.2 & 4.3).

**Table 4.1: Chronological events of reproductive phenophases (emergence of inflorescence primordia to dehiscence of the seed pod).**

| *Species* | *Emergence of inflorescence primordia (month)* | *Initiation to Anthesis (days)* | *Flowering time (month)* | *Longevity of individual flower (days)* | *Pod initiation pollination (days)* | *Browning of seed pod (months)* | *Dehiscence of seed pod (months)* |
|---|---|---|---|---|---|---|---|
| *V. alpina* | May-Jun | 50 | Jul-Aug | 18 | 5 | Nov-Dec | Feb-Mar |
| *V. bicolor* | Feb-Mar | 48 | Mar-Apr | 22 | 7 | Dec-Jan | Mar-Apr |
| *V. coerulea* | Jul-Aug | 62 | Sep-Nov | 28 | 7 | Jul-Aug | Feb-Mar |
| *V. coerulescens* | Feb-Mar | 98 | Jun | 7 | 4 | Nov-Dec | Feb-Mar |
| *V. cristata* | Nov-Dec | 103 | Mar-Apr | 24 | 6 | Oct-Nov | Feb-Mar |
| *V. liouvillei* | Feb-Mar | 79 | Apr-May | 26 | 7 | Nov-Dec | Mar-Apr |
| *V. pumila* | Feb-Mar | 85 | May-Jun | 17 | - | - | - |
| *V. stangeana* | Feb-Mar | 63 | Apr-May | 24 | 5 | Nov-Dec | Mar-Apr |
| *V. tessellata* | Feb-Mar | 69 | Apr-Jun | 23 | 6 | Dec-Jan | Mar-Apr |
| *V. testacea* | Mar-Apr | 67 | May-June | 12 | 5 | Oct-Nov | Mar-Apr |

***Emergence of inflorescence primordia :*** The period for the emergence of inflorescence primordia for the species studied is as follows. For *V. bicolor*, V. coerulescens, *V. liouvillei*, *V. pumila*, *V. stangeana* and *V. tessellata* it was from February - March when the maximum temperature increased from 16.2°C to 21.5°C and the minimum increased form 7.0°C to 11.5°C; at the same time the average rainfall had increased

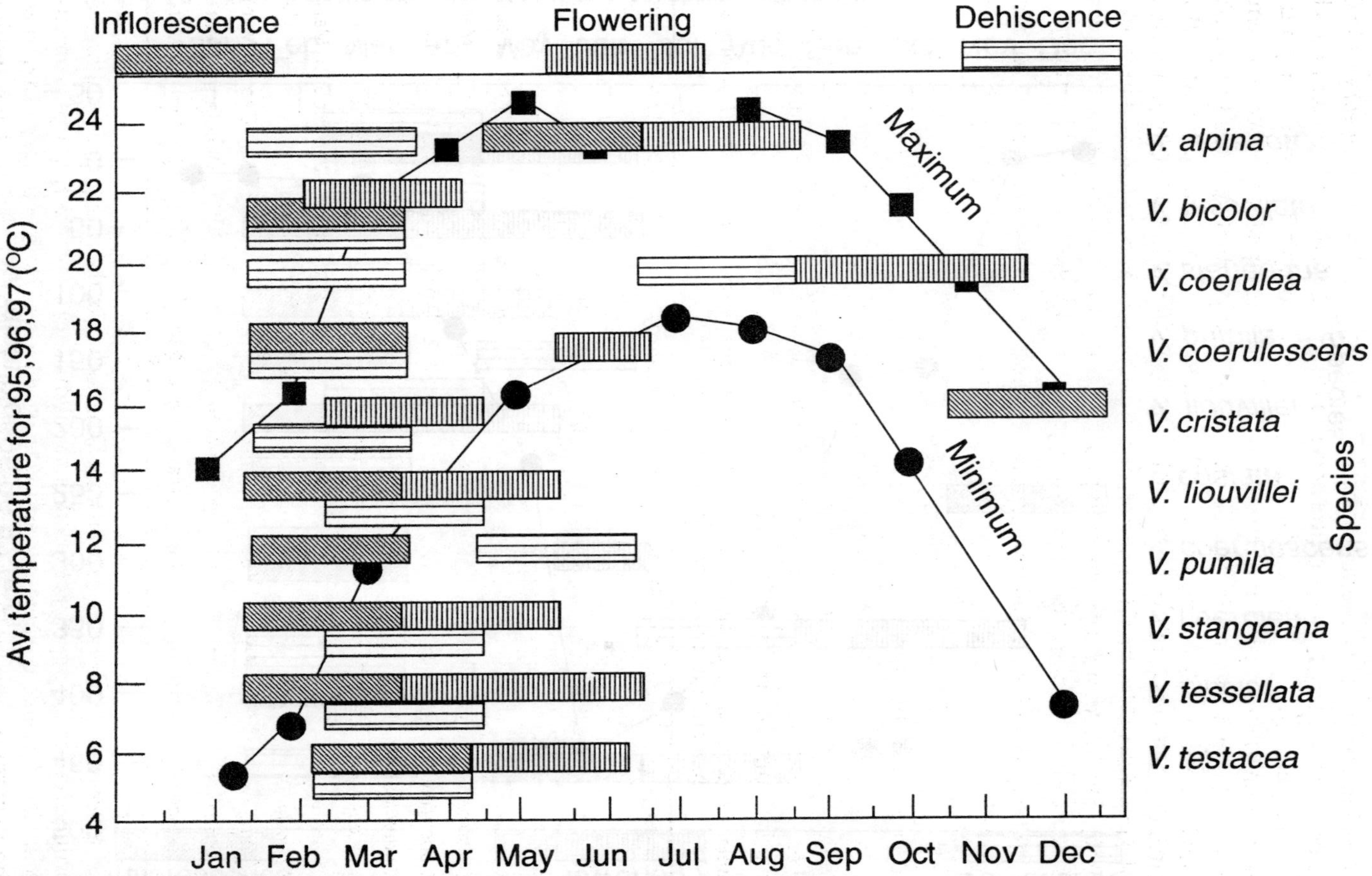


**Fig. 4.1: Chronological events of reproductive phenophases with temperature**

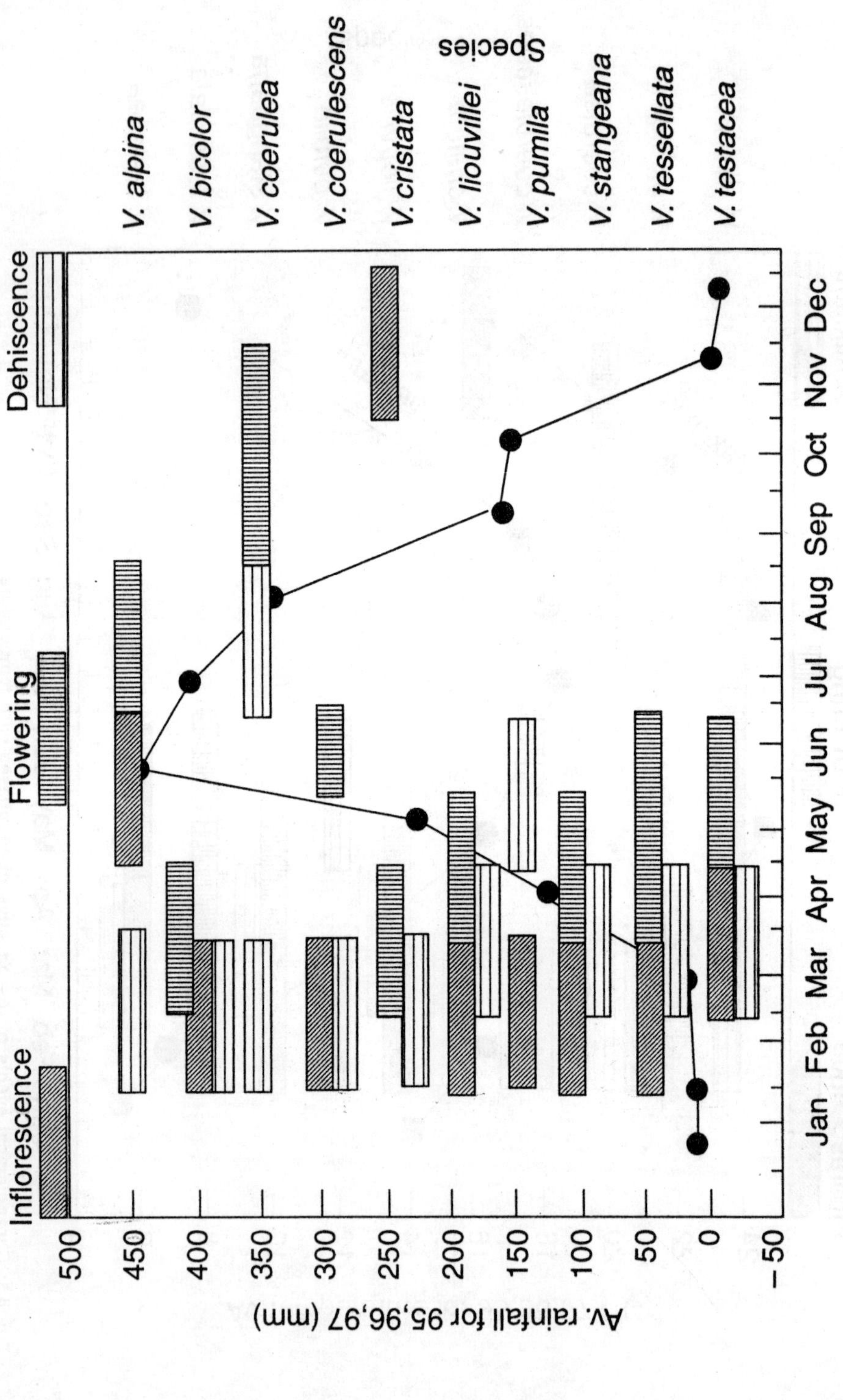


**Fig. 4.2: Chronological events of reproductive phenophases with rainfall**

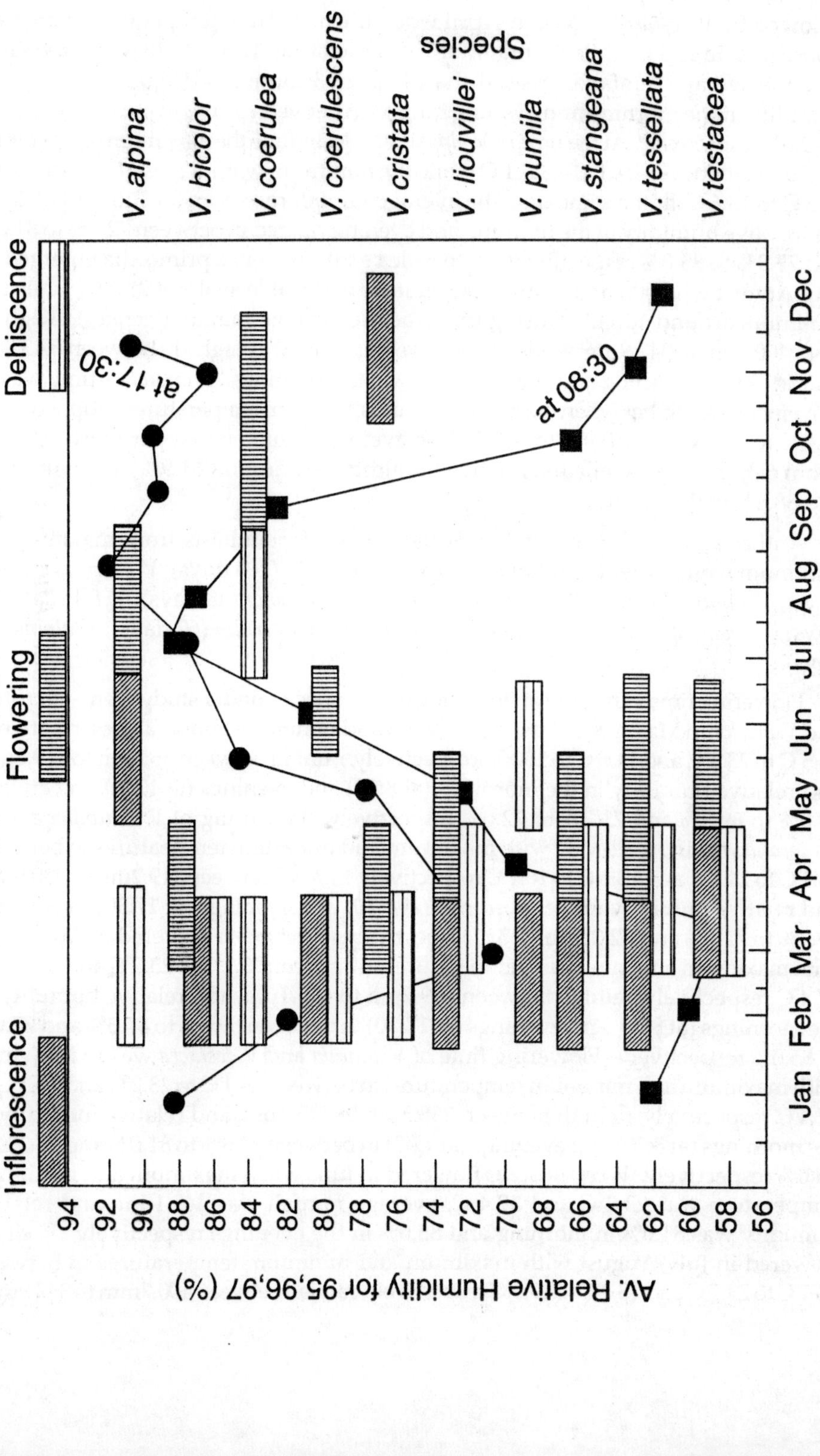


**Fig. 4.3: Chronological events of reproductive phenophases with relative humidity**

slightly from 19.7µm to 36.3µm. The relative humidity was falling, both in the morning and evening from 59.7% to 58.0% and from 81.7% to 71.3% respectively. These were followed by *V. testacea* in March-April when the maximum temperature increased from 21.5°C to 23.1°C while the minimum increased from 11.5°C to 13.6°C; at the same time the average rainfall increased sharply from 36.3µm to 119.2µm. The relative humidity in the morning and evening ranged in between 58.0% to 69.3% and 71.3% to 72.0% respectively. At the time of *V. alpina* i.e. in May-June the maximum temperature fluctuated between 24.1°C to 23.1°C while the minimum was increased slightly from 11.5°C to 13.6°C; at the same time the average rainfall rose from 36.3µm to 119.2µm. The relative humidity in the morning and evening ranged in between 72.3% to 81.0% and 77.3% to 85.0% respectively. V. coerulea's inflorescence primordia emerged in July-August when the maximum temperature was stable at about 23.6°C, while the minimum around 18.1°C. During this time the average rainfall decreased slightly from 400.7µm to 347.9µm, while the relative humidity was high - in between 87.3% to 82.8%% int he morning and 87.0% to 91.7% in the evenings. *V. cristata*'s time was in November-December when the maximum and minimum temperatures dropped from 19.2°C to 15.8°C and 10.9°C to 7.4°C. The average rainfall had a very low value of about 6.3µm. Meanwhile the relative humidity was around 61.9% in the morning and 88.8% in the evenings.

Anthesis period : The number of days taken for anthesis from maximum to minimum were under the following order. *V. cristata* (103 days), *V. coerulescens* (98 days), *V. pumila* (85 days), *V. liouvillei* (79 days), *V. bicolor* (48 days), *V. tessellata* (69 days), *V. testacea* (67 days), *V. stangeana* (63 days), *V. coerulea* (62 days), *V. alpina* (50 days).

Flowering time : The time of flowering for the species under study were - *V. cristata* and *V. bicolor* in March-April with maximum and minimum temperatures in between 21.5°C to 23.1°C and 11.5°C to 13.6°C respectively, rainfall between 36.3µm to 119.2µm, and relative humidity in the mornings (at 8:30) and evenings (at 17:30) in between 59.0% to 69.3% and 71.3% to 72.0% respectively. Flowering of *V. liouvillei* and *V. stangeana* was in April-May with maximum and minimum tempeatures in between 23.1°C to 24.1°C and 13.6°C to 16.1°C respectively, rainfall between 119.2µm to 238.5µm, and relative humidity in the mornings (at 8:30) and evenings (at 17:30) in between 69.3% to 72.3% and 72.0% to 77.3% respectively. *V. tessellata* flowered in April-June with maximum and minimum temperatures in between 23.1°C to 23.2°C and 13.6°C to 17.4°C respectively, rainfall between 119.2µm to 445.1µm, and relative humidity in the mornings (at 8:30) and evenings (at 17:30) in between 69.3% to 81.3% and 72.0% to 85.0% respectively. Flowering time of *V. pumila* and *V. testacea* was in May-June with maximum and minimum temperatures in between 24.1°C to 23.2°C and 16.1°C to 17.4°C respectively, rainfall between 238.5µm to 445.1µm, and relative humidity in the mornings (at 8:30) and evenings (at 17:3) in between 72.3% to 81.0% and 77.3% to 85.0% respectively. *V. coerulescens* flowered in June when maximum and minimum temperature was 23.2°C and 17.4°C, average rainfall was 445.1µm, and relative humidity was 81.0% in morning and 85.0% in the evenings respectively. *V. alpina* flowered in July-August with maximum and minimum temperatures in between 23.2°C to 23.7°C and 18.2°C to 17.9°C respectively, rainfall between 400.7mm to 347.9mm, and relative humidity in the mornings (at 8:30) and evenings (at 17:30) in between 87.3% to 82.8% and 87.0% to 91.7% respectively. *V. coerulea* flowered in September-November when maximum and minimum temperature was 23.2°C to 17.1°C, average rainfall was 171.4µm, and relative humidity was 81.0% in morning and 85.0% in the evenings respectively.

Longevity of individual flower : The longevity of the individual flowers (Fig. - 4.4) as observed were - *V. coerulea* (28 days), *V. liouvillei* (26 days), *V. cristata* and *V. stangeana* (24 days), *V. tessellata* (23 days), *V. bicolor* (22 days), *V. alpina* (18 days), *V. pumila* (17 days), *V. testacea* (12 days), *V. coerulescens* (7 days).

Seed pod initiation after pollination : The number of days from pollination to initiation were - *V. bicolor, V. coerulea* and *V. liouvillei* (7 days); *V. cristata* and *V. tessellata* (6 days); V alpina, *V. stangeana* and *V. testacea* (5 days); *V. coerulescens* (4 days). However, in the case of *V. pumila* fruiting failure was encountered.

Browning of the seed pod : Browning of the seed pod for *V. cristata* and *V. testacea* occured in the October-November with maximum and minimum temperatrues in between 21.5°C to 19.2°C and 14.1°C to 10.9°C respectively, rainfall between 166.0mm to 6.1mm, and relative humidity in the mornings (at 8:30) and evenings (at 17:30) were 62.8% to 90.0% respectively. For *V. alpina, V. coerulescens, V. liouvillei* and *V. stangeana* it occurred during November-December with maximum and minimum temperatures in between 19.2°C to 15.8°C and 10.9°C to 7.4°C respectivley, rainfall at around 6.32mm, and relative humidity in the mornings (at 8:30) and evenings (at 17:30) in between 62.8% to 60.4% and 86.8% to 90.7% respectively. For *V. bicolor* and *V. tessellata* it occurred during December-January with maximum and minimum temperatures in between 15.8°C and 14.1°C and 7.4°C and 5.1°C respectively, rainfall between 6.6mm to 16.9mm, and relative humidity in the mornings (at 8:30) and evenings (at 17:30) in between 60.4% to 61.7% and 90.7% to 88.0% respectively. Browning of seed pod for *V. coerulea* was in July-August with maximum and minimum temperatures at around 23.5°C and 18.1°C respectively, rainfall between 400.7mm to 347.9mm, and relative humidity in the mornings (at 8:30) and evenings (at 17:30) in between 87.3% to 82.8% and 87.0% to 91.7% respectively.

Dehiscence of seed pod : The time of dehiscence of the seed pod for *V. alpina, V. coerulea, V. coerulescens* and *V. cristata* were found to take place from February to March; whereas in the case of *V. bicolor, V. liouvillei, V. stangeana, V. tessellata* and *V. testacea* it occurs from March to April.

## Discussion

In a majority of the *Vandas* studied, viz.; *V. bicolor, V. coerulescens, V. liouvillei, V. pumila, V. stangeana* and *V. tessellata*, flower bud emerges during February-March followed by *V. testacea, V. alpina* and *V. coerulea* in the successive months of the year. After a gap of two months (September and October) *V. cristata* initiates flower bud (Novermber-December). Therefore, it is apparent that most species initiates flower bud when the days are shorter and the nights cold. It is generally believed that mnay orchid species are induced by, or promoted to flower by low temperature (Kosugi, 1952; Leffring, 1972; Kronenberg, 1976). On the other hand, *V. alpina* and *V. coerulea* initiates flower bud during the long days of mid-summer. Normally long day plants

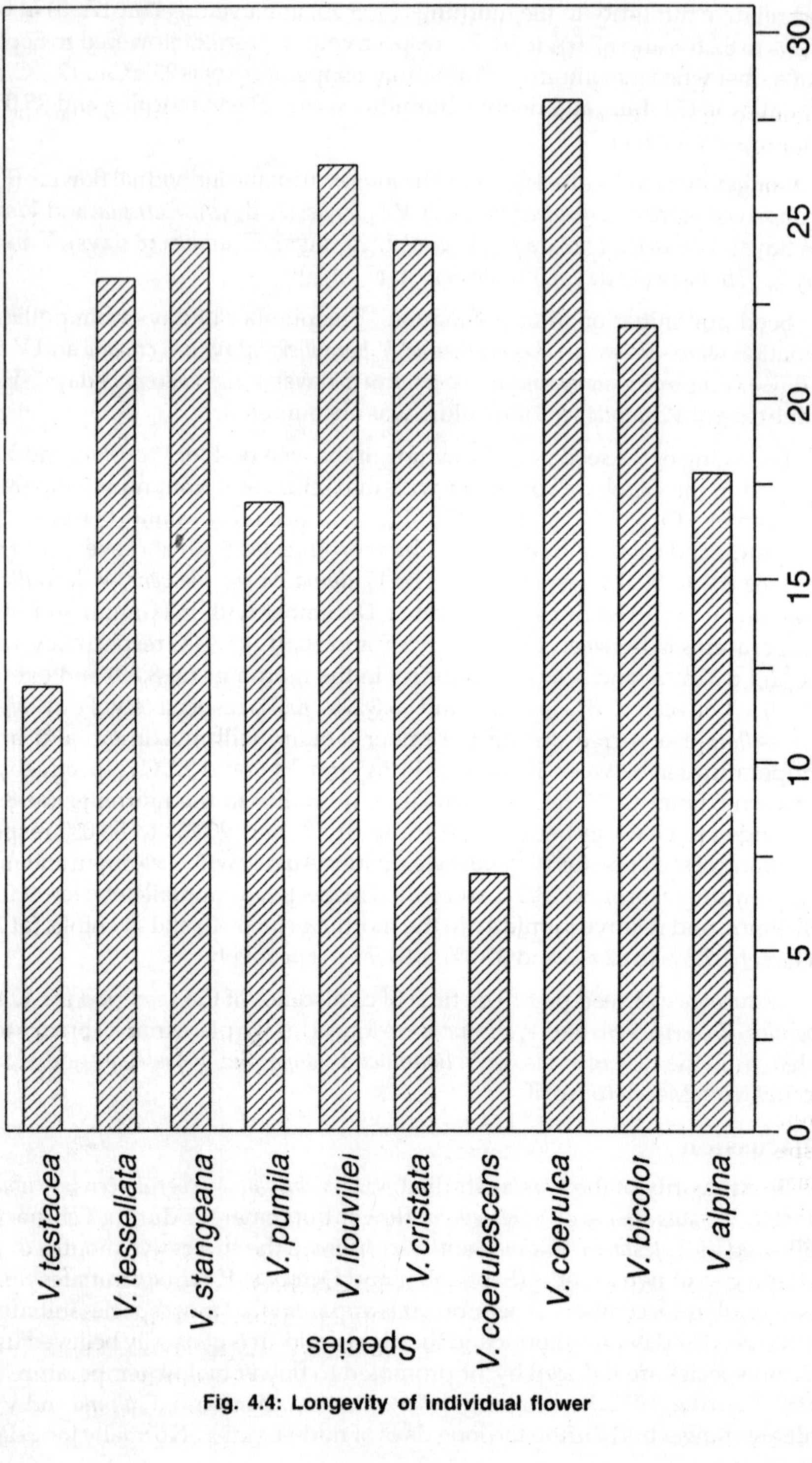


**Fig. 4.4: Longevity of individual flower**

flower in the autumn which is observed for *V. coerulea*, but for *V. alpina* this does not happen. The time from the emergence of inflorescence primordia to the opening of the flowers differ from species to species. Bose and Yadav (1986) have also stated that - floral initiation in orchids is determined by genotype and its development is in interaction with the environmental conditions. However, the above mentioned pattern certainly reflects the different phenological requirements among the species of Indian *Vandas*.

The peak flowering time for most of the species, viz.; *V. bicolor, V. coerulescens, V. liouvillei, V. pumila, V. cristata, V. stangeana, V. tessellata* and *V. testacea* is in April-June. All these species flower during spring and ealry summer, exception being *V. alpina* and and *V. coerulea* flowering in late summer and the autumn season. These two categories of flowering seasons can be broadly correlated to temperature and photoperiod respectively. As has been suggested by Jackson (1966), spring and early summer floweirng species are most closely correlated with temperature, while late summer and autumn flowering species are more closely correlated with photoperiod. Despite this generalization, the variation of the flowering season among the species reveals their optimum requirements for temperature, photoperiod, rainfall and relative humidity, besides the genetic factors. Natural selection may also act on plants to synchronize flowering phenology with periods of pollinator availability (Waser, 1979; Thompson, 1980). On the other hand, it may be related to the plant growing season (Zimmerman and Aide, 1989) or to environmental factors (Melampy, 1987; Wright, 1991).

The longevity of an individual flower in all the species is usually 1 to 4 weeks except in *V. coerulescens* and *V. testaceae*. These two species possess thin perianth parts and comparatively smaller flower size. The rest of the species possess fleshy perianth parts which may be contributing to their flower longevity. It has also been assumed that flower life spans are likely to be an adaptive characteristic (Heather & Lawrence, 1995).

The activity of seed pod settig and maturation is the longest phenophase. During the process of the seed pod developments it turns green in colour which could be for providing photosynthetic energy to developing seed. Browning of the seed pod takes place from October to January in all species except in *V. coerulea*. In this species browning coincides with the coming year inflorescence initiation in July-August. Therefore, the longest phenophase for seed maturation and retention is exhibited by this species. Irrespective of the differences in the browning period and time taken for the maturation of the seed, dehiscence of the seed pod occurs from February till April providing a better chance for wind dispersal when the strong dry winds blow in the region.

From these phenological study, the hybridizers can glean an essential information to orchid culture. These data on plant phenology can be used for scientific multiplication, propagation and also for conservation of germplasm.

# Chapter - 5
# Palynology

The science of Palynology implies the study of pollen grain and spore. Pollen grain houses the male grametophytic generation of the angiosperm and gymnosperm. The spores on the other hand is a resting and dispersal phase of the cryptogam. Although pollen grain and spore differ considerably in their function, they are both products from the meiotic cell division, surrounded by tough, resistant walls which are usually sculptured in distinctive ways.

Modern palynology chiefly springs from pollen morphology, pollen analysis and palaeobotany. A comparative analytical study of pollen morphology and wall structure can provide data for systematic phylogenetic utility. The importance of pollen morphology in the plant taxonomy was first emphasized by Radlkofer (1883) in his studies on the Acanthaceae, a family known for great beauty of its pollen grains.

Plant taxonomists are concerned to establish evolutionary relationship between extant plant populations and to classify these into particular level of organization where pollen grains and spores have an important part to play (Moore, et.al., 1991). In many instances the type of pollen of a taxon is characteristic and constant. Further, Nair (1985) opines that, the morphological characters of pollen grains and spores are important diagnostic criteria in consideration of taxonomy and inter-relationship of plants at various taxonomic levels. The taxonomic and evolutionary importance of pollen grain studies may be at family,. genus or species, and in certain cases even to their infra specific units.

In Angiosperms the morphological diversity of the exine, apertures and their surface sculpturing form the essential basis of present day palynology. According to Naik (1984) the main characters of taxonomic value in pollen grain studies are - (1) Number and position of furrows, (2) Number, position & complexity of apertures, (3) Form of exine sculpturing.

The importance of pollen morphology in taxonomy of orchidaceae was realised since the 18th century. The characters associated with pollinium has been one of the most importnat criterion and widely used in the classification of orchidaceae. The pollen grains of the orchidaceae exhibit remarkable diversity in their mode of organisation. The pollen may appear either as monads or are clustered together as different types of tetrads forming the pollinia. Orchids constitute the only group which contains all these types of associations. For instance, the supposely primitive diandrous species exhibit only monads, where the more advanced monandrous orchids show tetrads, massulae or pollinia. Thus the pattern of associaotn of pollen can certainly be used as a reliably criterion in classifactory and phylogenetic considerations in the orchidaceae. Within the orchidaceae, the stratification and sculpturing of the exine have been found to be extremely variable, although the tectate exine predominates (Kapil & Arora, 1990). The diversity in the nature and number of pollen apertures has been studied by workers like (Schill & Pfeiffer, 1977; Newton & Williams, 1978; Kapil & Arora, 1990).

The sarcanthinae and particulalry true *Vanda* is a complex and difficult group in need of a taxonomic revision. There have been several attempts to segregate, transfer and merger of species (Kumar *et al.*, 1997). In the light of such existing problem present status of controversial taxa deserve investigation with interdisciplinary approach. Palynotaxonomic (Palynological) studies might help in solving taxonomic problem as well as a better understanding of such groups.

A good deal of palynological literature has been contributed by various workers (Wodehose 1935; Erdtman, 1952; Nair, 1991; etc.) As early as 1969, Erdtman recommended that apertural condition and sporoderm stratification in pollen of orchids needs to be investigated more closely. But with regard to the palynology of orchids, only a few publication give any details about the pollen aperture in orchids and a few publications have recently appeared on temperate and a few tropical species (Arora, 1995). Therefore, in the present work it is attempted to study the number of pollinia, pollen organisation, size and shape, apertures and sculpturing of the exine in Indian species of the *Vanda*.

## Materials and Methods

Pollinium of *Vanda* was collected from the experimental orchid net house, Botany Department, NEHU, Shillong.

For Scanning Electron Microscope (SEM) studies, the pollinia were dissected out from the fresh flowers and dehydrated in ethanol seires, air-dried or directly mounted on copper stubs using double side sticky tape. The specimen were then sputter-coated with gold palladium alloy. Then the same was examined and photographed under JEOL-35 JSM CF scanning electron microscrope at an accelerating voltage of 15 KV. The characters studied with SEM were : Pollinium surface structure, exine sculpturing of pollen grains and type of aperture.

For Light Microscope (LM) studies, pollinia were placed on a clean slide and crushed with the help of a needle followed by staining with safranin and then photographed under suitable magnification. Polar and equatorial measurements were also recorded with the help of a ocular scale at 10X. A minimum of 20 fully developed grains were measured. The parameters studied with LM were shape and size of pollen grains and pollen tetrads. The shape of pollen grains were determined as prolate and subprolate basing on the value of the polar-equatorial ratios following Eardtman (1952). If the value was 1.33 to 2.00, it was considered as prolate, and if the value was 1.14 to 1.33 the shape was considered as subprolate.

## Results and Observations

During the present palynological studies in the Indian species of *Vanda*, it was observed that the pollen grains are organised into 2 distinct pollinia. These pollinia consist of two unequal lobes which is evident when the photograph (SEM) was taken focussing the two smaller lobes (Plate- 5.1, 5.6 5.7 5,10). The pollinia along with accessory structures, such as viscidium, caudicle and stipe has also been observed (Plate - 5.4 & 5.5).

Scanning Electron Microscope revealed that in all the species studied, the pollen grains were compactly packed together within the pollinium (Plate - 5.1 to 5.10). With respect to the pollen surface pattern - *V. alpina, V. bicolor, V. coerulea, V. coerulescens, V. pumila. V. tessellata* and *V. testacea* exhibited smooth or the so called psilate, whereas in *V. cristata, V. liouvillei* and *V. stangeana* they were foveolate (with holes and depressions).

In all the species examined, pollen grains were found to be aperturate. Majority of the species were monoaperturate and the aperture occupies more or less the central position. But in the case of *V. bicolor* and *V. coerulea* biaperaturate condition was observed (Plate - 5.2c & 5.3c). Under higher magnification the shape of the aperture appeared irregular in outline (Plate - 5.1c to 5.10c). However, in all the species the aperatures seemed to be irregularly shaped pori (isodiametric aperatures with slightly elongated and roundish ends).

Detailed examination under Light Microscope revealed that the pollen grains were aggregated together as different forms of tetrads within the pollinium. They are - decussate, rhomboidal, tetrahedral and linear (Plate - 5.1d to 5.10d). The dimension of tetrads varied from species to species (Table - 5.1). Consideraing the polar/equatorial value, *V. coerulea* had the largest dimension (3.257 x 2.074 $\mu m^2$) while *V. coerulescens* had the smallest (2.138 x 1.370 $\mu m^2$). Measurement of individual pollen grains evaluated for their shape category are provided in Table - 5.1. Basing on the polar/equatorial ratios pollen grains were found to be sub-prolate in *V. alpina, V. bicolor, V. coerulescens, V. liouvillei, V. pumila, V. stangeana,* and *V. testacea* while in *V. coerulea, V. cristata* and V. tessellate the pollens were prolate.

**Table - 5.1 : Tetrad and single pollen grains measurement**

| *Species* | *Tetrad (µm)* | | | *Single (µm)* | | | *Shape* |
|---|---|---|---|---|---|---|---|
| | *P/sd* | *E/sd* | *P/E* | *P/sd* | *E/sd* | *P/E* | |
| *V. alpina* | 2.97/0.46 | 2.01/0.40 | 1.48 | 1.11/0.20 | 0.91/0.11 | 1.22 | sub-prolate |
| *V. bicolor* | 2.68/0.35 | 1.96/0.26 | 1.37 | 1.08/0.15 | 0.82/0.13 | 1.32 | sub-prolate |
| *V. coerulea* | 3.25/0.39 | 2.07/0.26 | 1.57 | 1.32/0.23 | 0.99/0.10 | 1.33 | prolate |
| *V. coerulescens* | 2.14/0.43 | 1.45/0.26 | 1.48 | 1.07/0.12 | 0.82/0.12 | 1.30 | sub-prolate |
| *V. cristata* | 2.94/0.21 | 1.97/0.16 | 1.49 | 1.22/0.17 | 0.91/0.15 | 1.34 | prolate |
| *V. liouvillei* | 3.24/0.46 | 2.01/0.31 | 1.61 | 1.24/0.22 | 0.99/0.12 | 1.25 | sub-prolate |
| *V. pumila* | 3.14/0.28 | 2.34/0.28 | 1.34 | 1.14/0.23 | 0.88/0.09 | 1.30 | sub-prolate |
| *V. stangeana* | 2.88/0.44 | 1.97/0.32 | 1.46 | 1.17/0.22 | 0.90/0.11 | 1.30 | sub-prolate |
| *V. tessellata* | 2.84/0.28 | 1.88/0.22 | 1.51 | 1.11/0.13 | 0.83/0.11 | 1.34 | prolate |
| V. testacea | 2.66/0.38 | 1.86/0.19 | 1.43 | 1.06/0.10 | 0.86/0.10 | 1.23 | sub-prolate |

sd - standard deviation; P/E - Polar/Equatorial

## Discussion

Present investigation have shown that the number of pollinia was two in all species. The pollinium number is usually uniform within the genera and possibly with subtribe and tribe (Freudenstein & Rasmussen, 1996). Dressler (1981) and Rasmussen (1985) considered that many of the genera with two pollinia are found in members of vandoid group. Furthermore, Burns-Balogh & Fank (1986), has proposed that the fusion of four sporogenous zone during the early stages of development was responsible for the production of two pollinia in the vandeae. The association of caudicle, stipe and viscidium has been discussed in detail by Dressler (1981) and suggested that these structures help during pollination.

In all the *Vanda* species examined, the pollen grains were in tetrads or massulae forming the pollinia which is an indication of advanced trait. The nature of pollen organization is an important feature in the orchidaceae. For instance in the primitive diandrous taxa the pollen are liberated as monads, whereas the more advanced monandrous orchids are in tetrads, massulae or pollinia (Ackerman & Williams, 1980; Arora, 1986).

With regard to the surface pattern of pollen, it varies from psilate to foveolate. The reason could be - exine structure have evolved in several directions because similar type is found in two very different group of orchids e.g. Orchidioideae and Epidendroideae as suggested by Burns-Balogh (1983). The aspect relating to the sculpturing of the pollen wall within the orchidaceae have been found to be extremely variable. In the tribe Cypripedeae and Neottieae, the exine is relatively uniform whereas in Orchideae and Epidendreae they are heterogenous (Kapil & Arora, 1990). According to Williams and Broome (1976) a psilate exine is characteristic of higher orchids with the exception of Cypripedioideae and the smooth surface of the most advanced is due to fusion of extosexine into a definite tectum. Arora (1985) have also suggested the more advanced orchids lack detailed sculpturing of the exine.

The present study revealed poroid grain in all the species which is in accord with the workers like Schill & Pfeffier (1977) and Newton & Williams (1978). They found that when the aperture is present, it is colpoid in Diandreae and poroid in Monandreae. However, Schill & Pfeiffer (1977), Ackerman & Williams (1980), Balogh (1982b), Yeung & Blackman (1983a) found that most of the members investigated by them were inaperaturate.

Different types of tetrads such as decussate rhomboidal, tetrahedral and linear, tetrad size and prolate to subprolate shaped pollen grains can certainly be a functional tool not only as supportive evidence for species concept, but also for evaluating relationship among species complexes.

From various information obtained in the pollen studies, evidently the characters viz.; two numbers of pollinia, psilate to foveolate surface pattern of pollens, organization of pollen grains inthe form of tetrads forming the pollinia and poroid type of apertures as was observed are characteristics of advanced orchids, and these were found consistent in all the species examined. Therefore, based on palynological study all the species studied can be placed in the same genus. It is opined that the erection of genera such as *Trudelia* Garay as a distinctive species was premature (Christenson, 1992). *Trudelia* in the sense of Garay is unnatural as it divides a cohesive species cluster. *Trudelia* has not been accepted as a distinct genus but its species are still considered under *Vanda*.

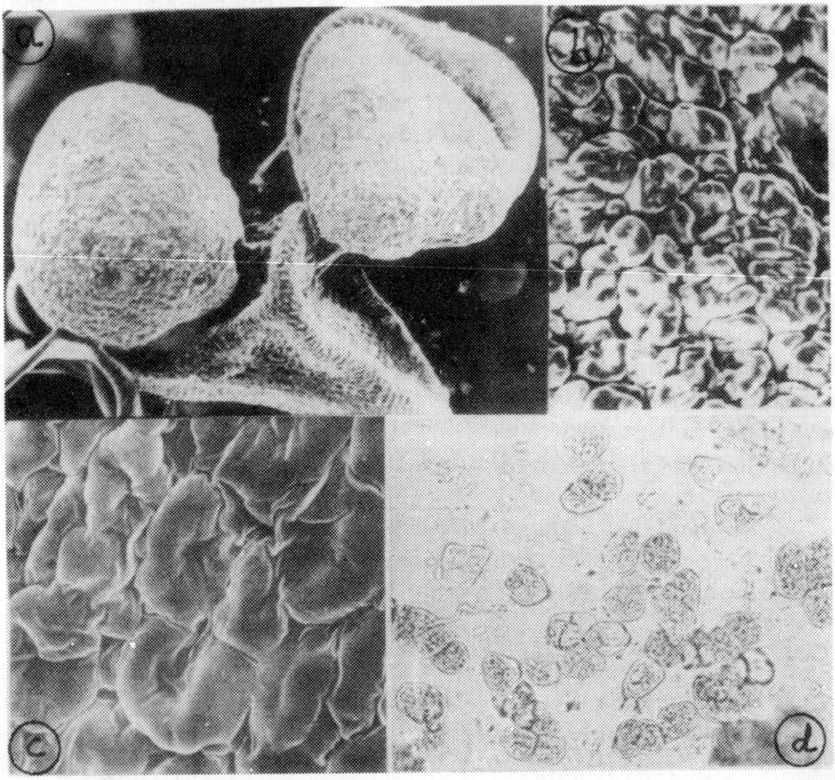


**Plate 5.1:** ***V. alpina***

**SEM**: (a) Pollinium – **X66**; (b) An enlarged portion showing pollen packing – **X540**; (c) Aperature at higher magnification – **X1200**;

**LM**: (d) Diffferent types of tetrads – **X25.**

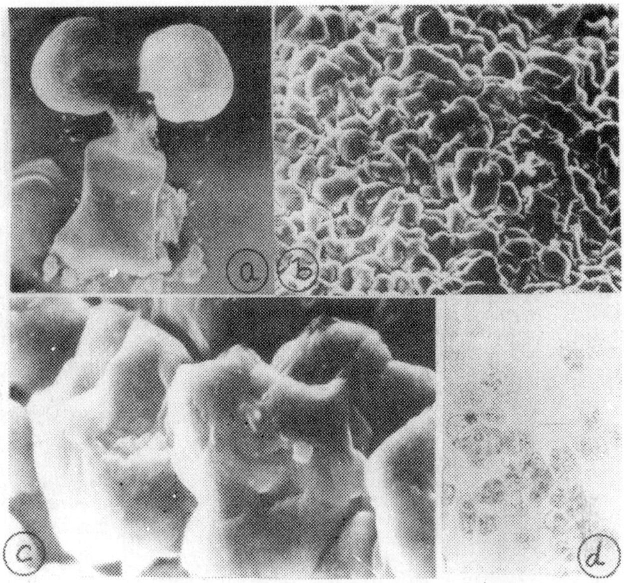

**Plate 5.2:** ***V. bicolor***

**SEM**: (a) Pollinium – **X26**; (b) An enlarged portion showing pollen packing – **X540**;
(c) Aperature at higher magnification – **X2400**;

**LM**: (d) Diffferent types of tetrads – **X25.**

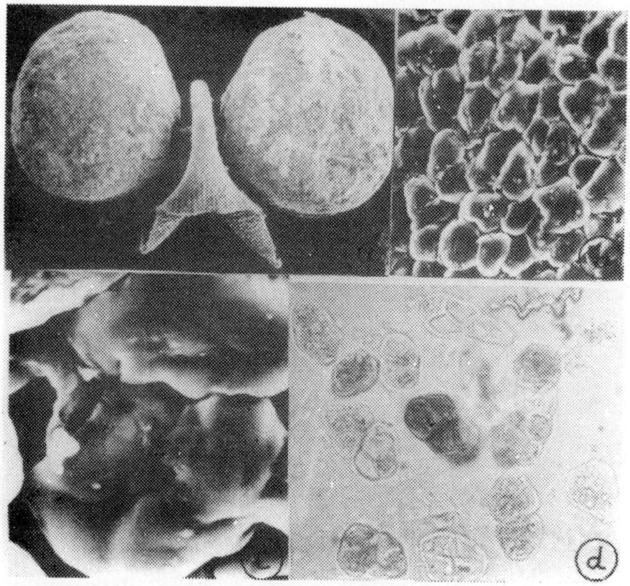

**Plate 5.3:** ***V. coerulea***

**SEM**: (a) Pollinium – **X39**; (b) An enlarged portion showing pollen packing – **X660**;
(c) Aperature at higher magnification – **X3000**;

**LM**: (d) Diffferent types of tetrads – **X40.**

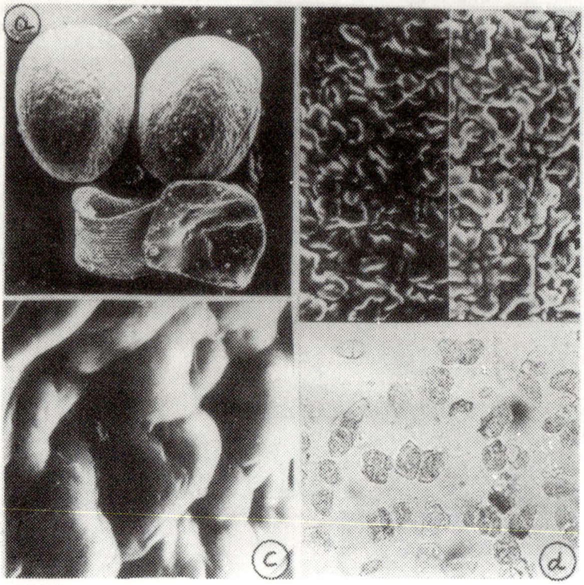

**Plate 5.4:** ***V. coerulescens***

**SEM:** (a) Pollinium – **X54**; (b) An enlarged portion showing pollen packing – **X540**; (c) Aperature at higher magnification – **X2600**;

**LM:** (d) Diffferent types of tetrads – **X25.**

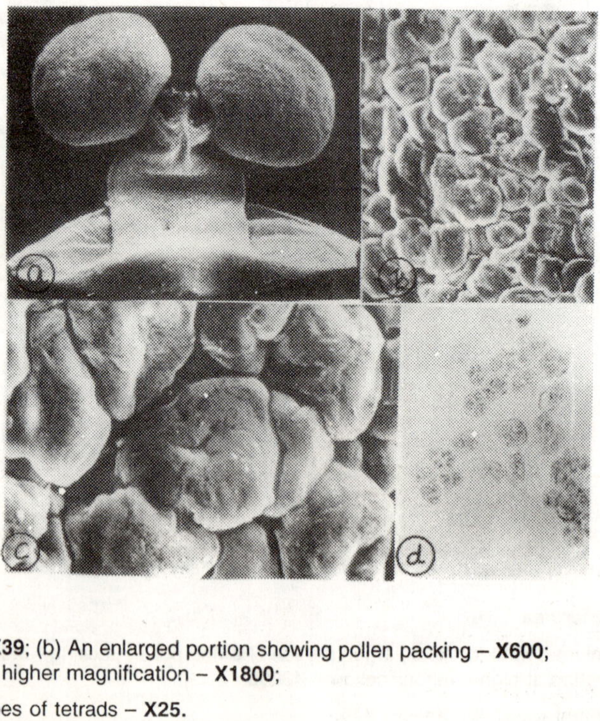

**Plate 5.5:** ***V. cristata***

**SEM:** (a) Pollinium – **X39**; (b) An enlarged portion showing pollen packing – **X600**; (c) Aperature at higher magnification – **X1800**;

**LM:** (d) Diffferent types of tetrads – **X25.**

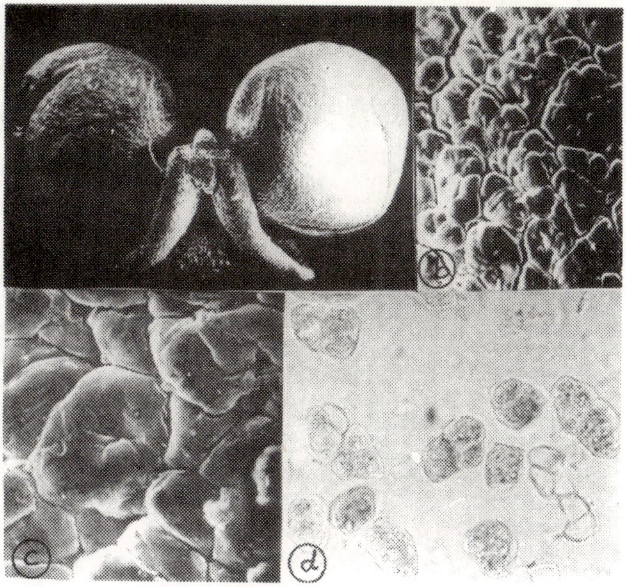


**Plate 5.6:** ***V. liouvillei***

**SEM**: (a) Pollinium – **X44**; (b) An enlarged portion showing pollen packing – **X440**; (c) Aperature at higher magnification – **X1600**;

**LM**: (d) Diffferent types of tetrads – **X40.**

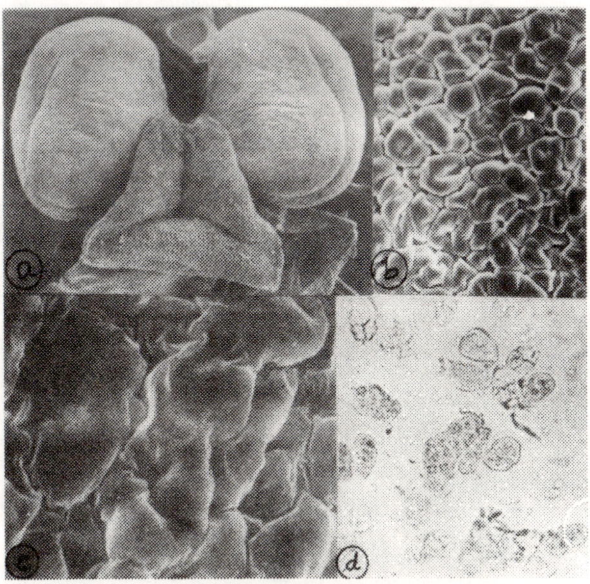


**Plate 5.7:** ***V. pumila***

**SEM**: (a) Pollinium – **X49**; (b) An enlarged portion showing pollen packing – **X500**; (c) Aperature at higher magnification – **X2000**;

**LM**: (d) Diffferent types of tetrads – **X25.**

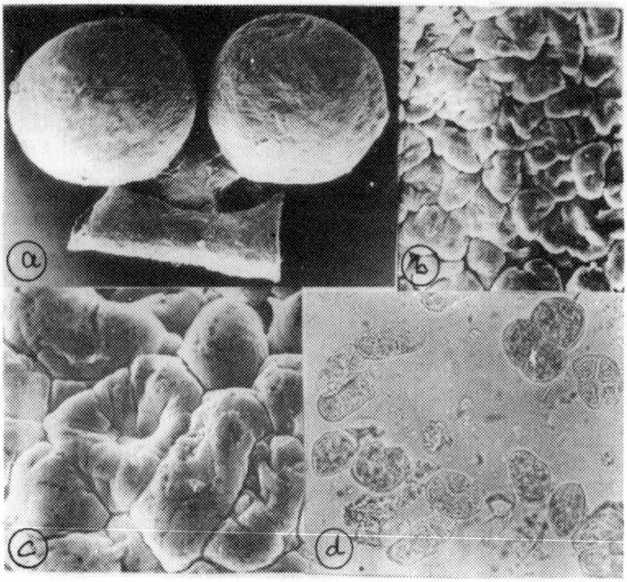

**Plate 5.8:** ***V. stangeana***

**SEM:** (a) Pollinium – **X44**; (b) An enlarged portion showing pollen packing – **X600**; (c) Aperature at higher magnification – **X1800**;

**LM:** (d) Diffferent types of tetrads – **X40.**

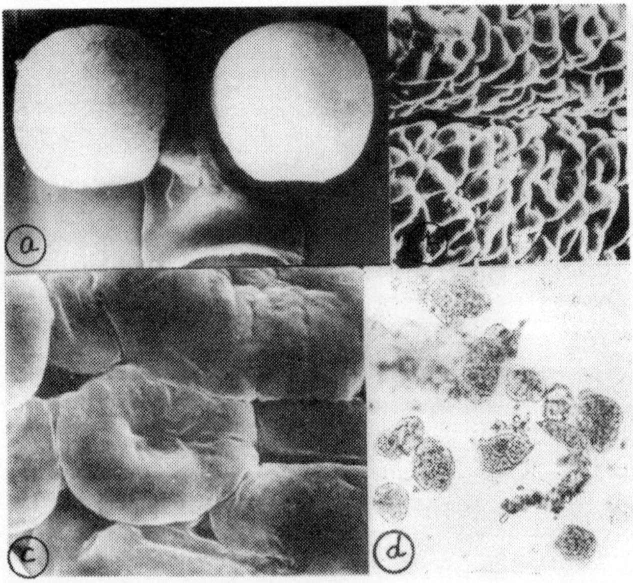

**Plate 5.9:** ***V. tessellata***

**SEM:** (a) Pollinium – **X36**; (b) An enlarged portion showing pollen packing – **X600**; (c) Aperature at higher magnification – **X2000**;

**LM:** (d) Diffferent types of tetrads – **X25.**

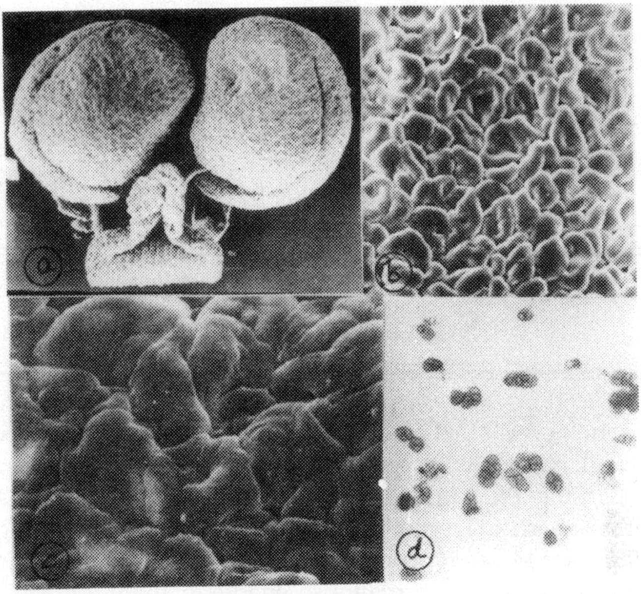

**Plate 5.10: *V. testacea***

**SEM**: (a) Pollinium – **X49**; (b) An enlarged portion showing pollen packing – **X600**;
(c) Aperature at higher magnification – **X1200**;

**LM**: (d) Diffferent types of tetrads – **X16.**

## Chapter - 6

# Seed Morphometry

Seed morphology was first pointed out for classification of orchidaceae by Clifford and Smith (1969). Subsequenlty, seed characters have been used to distinguish species (Haas, 1977; Bartholott & Ziegler, 1981; Healey *et al.*, 1980). There are several systems of classification of orchids based on conventional macromorphological characters (Dressler, 1981). However, for controversial taxon like *Vanda* additional taxonomic characters are required which may also enable in solving taxonomic problems. Morphometric studies using Scanning Electron Microscope (SEM) and Light Microscope (LM) can elucidate both systematic relationship and pattern of seed structures which can serve as taxonomic and phylogenetic markers. These may also explain certain aspects of seed biology (Barthlott, 1976).

Seed morphology serves as a relatively common source of systematic characters to circumscribe subgeneric gropus, or hypothesize relationship among species within a genus (Mathews and Levins, 1986; Ness, 1989). However, Barthlott (1981) has advocated that seed morphology is used less commonly to develop hypothesis about relationship among genera and other higher level taxa.

Orchid seeds are minute and vary considerably in size, morphology, structure and fine details. According to Molvray and Kores (1995), the shape of the orchid seed varies from filiform to fusiform, clavate to ellipsoidal, spindle shaped and sometimes permanently winged. The seed coat is derived solely from the outer integument and is uniseriate in all except for a few taxa. The number of cells that form the testa varies among different seed classes. Their size may be uniform or some cells may be noticeably larger or smaller within areas such as the middle region or the chalazal end. Anticlinal walls frequently appear strongly raised, whereas the outer periclinal surface is generally sunken or concave, giving the outer surface of the seed a tessellate appearance. The walls of the testa cells can be smooth or reticulated and when reticulation is present its pattern may be distinctive (Healey et at., 1980).

The embryos of different genera and species may vary in size, shape, colour and the ratios between their volumes. Orchid seeds consist of an oval shaped embryo generally enclosed within a transparent and often fusiform to oblong shaped testa (Arditt, *et al.*, 1967 & 1979; Beer, 1963). Healey *et al.*(1980) stated that, orchid embryos tend to be uniform in size within genera. However, the dimensions of testa may be more variable which led to an increase in the percentage of air space between the seed testa and embryo making the seed buoyant and aid in wind dispersion in the orchidaceae.

Barthlott and Zeigler's (1981) survey of the family orchidaceae recognises 20 different seed types based on overall seed shape, relative elongation of some cells in the seed coat, height and sculpturing of seed walls, and features of wall adhesion zone between adjacent cells, including the presence of intercellular gaps and beadings. Three of these seed types are - Orchis type, Disa-Diuris type and Goodyera type. These three types are further subdivided into sub types. However, many of the characters that define a particular seed type are not unique to it. As a result Dressler (1993) noted that Barthlott had recognised numerous intermediate between the Disa-Diuris type and Goodyera type in the recent years. Therefore, a more consistent interpretation of seed characters could assist in elucidating phylogenetic relationship in all the orchid genera.

Generally the main taxonomic value of orchid seed morphometry appear to be on the genus, sub tribe and tribe level. However, it can be used to distinguish between species and could be applied to phylogeny (Batthlott, 1976). For instance, in specific groups certain characters appear to be homologous and supportive of relatlionship trait. Furthermore, morphologically discernable groups can be identified by employing the seed characters.

Therefore, in the present investigation, studies on shape, size, surface structure of the seed and embryo dimensions in the Indian species of *Vanda* have been made.

## Materials and Methods

All the seeds examined were collected from the experimental orchid net house at Botany Department, NEHU, Shillong. The flowers were hand pollinated and harvested when the seed pod were fully matured. The seeds stored in small vials over $CaCl_2$ at 4°C in a desiccator were used for SEM and LM study.

Seed surface studies were recorded from observations done under Scanning Electron Microscope (SEM). The seeds wre mounted on aluminium copper stubs using double adhesive tape. The same were then sputter-coated with gold-palladium alloy for five minutes and photographed on a JEOL-35 JSMCF-SEM at an accelerating voltage of 15 KV.

Under the Light Microscope (LM) seed length and breadth, number of testa cells at the longest axis, embryo length and breadth were studied. The seed samples were stained with safranin and spread on a slide with a drop of distilled water and placed under a cover slip. They were photographed under suitable magnification. For each species, twenty seeds were measured along their longest and widest axis using an ocular micrometer scale at 10X and the average was calculated. The number of testa cells at the longest axis was also recorded. Colour of the seeds was described in subjective terms with the help of optical microscope.

For the calculation of seed and embryo volume, the method of Arditti *et al.* (1979) was employed as the shape of the seeds were fusiform and the embryo shape was prolate spheroid (Elliptical in cross section). The seed volume (fusiform shape) was calculated using the following formula,

Seed volume = 2{(π/3).(l/2).(w/2)2}

where,

π = 3.1416,
l = length,
w = width,
l/2 = h = height of each cone,
w/2 = r = radius of each cone,
(π/3).(w/2)2.(l/2) = (π/3).(r)2.(h) = volume of a cone of height *h*, radius *r*.

The embryo volume (prolate spheroid) is given as.

Embryo volume = (4/3).π.a.b2,

where,

a = half of embryo length,
b = half of embryo width.

## Results and Observations

Seed morphometric studies in the Indian species of *Vanda* revealed that the seeds were fusiform shaped (Plate - 6.1-6.9; Figs: a). The seed coats were transparent, uni-integumented and seed coat colour varied from (Table - 6.1) brown (*V. coerulescens, V. cristata, V. liouvillei, V. stangeana* and *V. tessellata*), golden brown (*V. bicolor* and *V. testacea*) to dark brown (*V. alpina* and *V. coerulea*). All the seed have an opening at the base. In all the cases, anticlinal cell walls appeared strongly raised and the cells were not uniform in size. The medial cells were more elongated whreas the micropylar and chalazal cells were much shorter (Plate - 6.1-6.9; Figs:b).

Scanning Electron Microscope examination revealved that the wall of testa cells were smooth and without any reticulation. However, under higher magnification (Plates - 6.1, 6.3, 6.5, 6.7 & 6.9; Figs.) some longitudinal folds were observed in *V. alpina* (x940), *V. coerulea* (x1000), *V. cristata* (x940), *V. liouvillei* (x1500), *V. stangeana* (x1300) and *V. testacea* (x1300).

The average number of testa cells along the longest axis of the seed were more than 2.00 in the case of *V. alpina* (2.01), *V. bicolor* (2.47), *V. coerulea* (2.06), *V. cristata* (2.47) and *V. stangeana* (2.07); and below 2.00 in case of *V. liouvillei* (1.93), *V. coerulescens* (1.53), *V. tessellata* (1.87) and *V. testacea* (1.93). The average length and width of the testa cells was also found to be species specific (Table - 6.1). Average length of testa cells were found to be maximum in *V. tessellata* (13.77) followed by *V. testacea* (11.90), *V. liouvillei* (11.41), *V. coerulescens* (11.07), *V. alpina* (10.20), *V. bicolor* (10.11), *V. stangeana* (9.59), V coerulea (9.18) and *V. cristata* (8.39).

The length of seeds varied from 16.52 μm to 27.52 μm. Maximum length was recorded with *V. cristata* and then further decrease was in the following order - *V. bicolor* > *V. tessellata* . *V. liouvillei* > V. coerulae > *V. stangeana* > *V. alpina* > *V. testacea* > *V. coerulescens*. The width of seed varied from 7.25 μm to 10.29 um. The width of seed was maximum to minimum was in the following order - *V. cristata* > *V. coerulea* > *V. tessellata* > V. liouvillei > *V. stangeana* = *V. bicolor* > *V. alpina* > *V. coerulescens* . *V. testacea.* When seed length is plotted against seed width the seed length varied more as compared to seed width (Fig. 6.1).

**Table 6.1 (a): Colours and numerical parameters of the observed seeds.**

| Species | Colour | Seed | | | | | | |
|---|---|---|---|---|---|---|---|---|
| | | Length l (μm/sd) | Width w (μm/sd) | length/ width | No. of cells at longest axis of testa | Average length of testa cells (μm) | Average width of testa cells (μm) | Volume ($\mu m^3$) |
| *V. alpina* | Dark Brown | 19.79/1.95 | 8.00/1.05 | 2.47 | 2.01 | 10.20 | 0.91 | 331.53 |
| *V. bicolor* | Golden Brown | 27.15/0.77 | 8.37/0.41 | 3.24 | 2.47 | 10.11 | 0.09 | 498.25 |
| *V. coerulea* | Dark Brown | 24.96/1.36 | 9.65/0.83 | 2.59 | 2.06 | 9.18 | 1.09 | 608.29 |
| *V. coerulescens* | Brown | 16.52/1.67 | 7.30/0.97 | 2.14 | 1.53 | 11.07 | 1.00 | 230.48 |
| *V. cristata* | Brown | 27.52/1.51 | 10.29/0.79 | 2.67 | 2.47 | 8.39 | 0.89 | 763.36 |
| V. liouvelli | Brown | 25.49/2.20 | 8.59/0.64 | 2.97 | 1.93 | 11.41 | 1.40 | 492.09 |
| *V. stangeana* | Brown | 21.33/0.94 | 8.37/0.51 | 2.55 | 2.07 | 9.59 | 1.41 | 391.58 |
| *V. tessellata* | Brown | 27.04/1.18 | 9.60/0.86 | 2.82 | 1.87 | 13.77 | 0.86 | 652.41 |
| *V. testacea* | Golden Brown | 18.61/1.30 | 7.25/0.56 | 2.57 | 193. | 11.90 | 1.33 | 256.37 |

sd - standard deviation

**Table 6.1(b): Numerical parameters of the observed embryos**

| Species | Embryo | | | | | |
|---|---|---|---|---|---|---|
| | Length a' (μm/sd) | Width b' (μm/sd) | Length/ width | Volume ($\mu m^3$) | Seed vol / Embryo vol | Percentage of air sapce $\frac{\text{Seed vol - Embryo vol}}{\text{Seed vol}} \times 100$ |
| *V. alpina* | 11.36/1.95 | 6.40.0.86 | 1.78 | 243.63 | 1.36 | 26.51 |
| *V. bicolor* | 18.29/0.79 | 6.56/0.33 | 2.79 | 42.19 | 1.21 | 17.27 |
| *V. coerulea* | 16.80/1.17 | 7.79/0.88 | 2.16 | 533.35 | 1.14 | 12.41 |
| *V. coerulescens* | 14.68/1.60 | 5.28/0.59 | 2.78 | 214.32 | 1.08 | 7.01 |
| *V. cristata* | 16.27/1.72 | 8.75/0.93 | 1.94 | 679.38 | 1.12 | 11.00 |
| V. liouvellei | 18.29/1.45 | 6.35/0.47 | 2.88 | 385.82 | 1.28 | 21.60 |
| *V. stangeana* | 14.56/1.46 | 6.88/0.66 | 2.12 | 360.86 | 1.09 | 7.85 |
| *V. tessellata* | 18.45/1.26 | 7.68/0.66 | 2.40 | 569.90 | 1.14 | 12.65 |
| *V. testacea* | 14.24/1.25 | 5.60/0.52 | 2.54 | 233.82 | 1.10 | 8.80 |

sd - standard deviation

The length/width ratio decreased from maximum of 3.24 in the following order - *V. bicolor* > *V. liouvillei* > V. tessellata > *V. cristata* > *V. coerulea* > *V. testacea* > *V. stangeana* > *V. alpina* > *V. coerulescens*. The seed length/seed width when plotted against respective species (Fig - 6.2) revealed that the decrease in the ratio value from maximum to minium was in the following order - *V. bicolor* (3.24) > *V. liouvillei* (2.97)

> V. tessellata (2.82) > *V. cristata* (2.67) > *V. coerulea* (2.59) > *V. testacea* (2.57) > *V. stangeana* (2.55) . *V. alpina* (2.47) > *V. coerulescens* (2.14). These value reveal the relative degree of truncation. Truncation of seeds is inversely proportionate to length/width ratio (Table - 6.1a).

Maximum seed volume recorded was 763.36 $\mu m^3$ (*V. cristata*) and minimum was 230.48 $\mu m^3$ (*V. coerulescens*). The decrease in seed volume in different species of *Vanda* was in the following order - *V. cristata* > *V. tessellata* > *V. coerulea* . *V. bicolor* > *V. liouvillei* > *V. stangeana* . *V. alpina* > *V. testacea* > *V. coerulescens.*

In case of embryo dimensions, the length decreased from maximum (18.36μm) to minimum (11.36μm) in the following order - V. tessellatea > *V. liouvillei* > *V. bicolor* . *V. coerulea* > *V. cristata* . *V. coerulescens* > *V. stangeana* > *V. testacea* > *V. alpina.* The width from maximum (8.75um) to minimum (5.28um) decreased in the following order - *V. cristata* > *V. coerulea* > *V. tessellata* > *V. stangeana* > *V. bicolor* > *V. alpina* . *V. liouvillei* > *V. testacea* > *V. coerulescens.* When embryo length was plotted against embryo width, variation was found to be more in embryo length but less so in embryo width (Fig. - 6.3). Length to width ratios varied from maximum in *V. liouvillei* (2.88) to minimum in *V. alpina* (1.78) in the following order - *V. liouvillei* (2.88), *V. bicolor* (2.79), *V. coerulescens* (2.78), *V. testacea* (2.54), *V. tessellata* (2.40), *V. coerulea* (2.16), *V. stangeana* (2.12), *V. cristata* (1.94), *V. alpina* (1.78). Embryo volume was found to be largest in *V. cristata* (679.38$\mu m^3$) and decreasing order was as follows - *V. tessellata* (569.90$\mu m^3$), *V. coerulea* (533.35$\mu m^3$), *V. bicolor* (412.19$\mu m^3$), *V. liouvillei* (385.82$\mu m^3$), *V. stangeana* (360.86$\mu m^3$), *V. alpina* (243.63$\mu m^3$), *V. testacea* (233.82$\mu m^3$) and *V. coerulescens* (214.32$\mu m^3$).

Seed to embryo volume ratios was observed to be highest in *V. alpina* (1.36) and it decreased in the following order - *V. liouvillei* (1.28), *V. bicolor* (1.21), *V. coerulea* (1.14), *V. tessellata* (1.14), *V. cristata* (1.12), *V. testacea* (1.10), *V. stangeana* (1.09) and *V. coerulescens* (1.08). The difference in these rations among the species were directly correlated to the percentage of air space present in the seeds (Fig. - 6.4). The percentage of air space was observed to be maximum in *V. alpina* (26.51%) and the decrease in air space was found n the following order - *V. liouvillei* (21.60%), *V. bicolor* (17.27%), *V. tessellata* (12.65%), *V. coerulea* (12.41%), V cristata (11.00%), *V. testacea* (8.80%), *V. stangeana* (7.85%) and *V. coerulescens* (7.01%).

When seed volume was plotted against embryo volume (Fig. - 6.5) it was revealed that as the seed volumes increased the embryo volume also increased.

## Discussion

A considerable uniformity in the shape of the seeds (fusiform) as well as the arrangement of testa cells i.e. long medial, short apical and chalazal cells along the longest axis suggest affinites with respect to seed characters among the Indian species of the *Vanda*. Molvray & Kore (1995) has also observed the similar type in orchidioid seeds where highly elongate medial cells with abrupt transition between small, isodiametric end cells. This type was also very close to Barthlott & Zeigler (1981) orchis-type. Further, orchis-type is said to have elongate medial cells, thin and high anticlinal cell wall without intercellular gaps (Zeigler, 1981). It is evident from the present investigation that in all Indian species of *Vanda* closely similar trait was exhibited and hence this could be attributed to the orchids type.

The structure and form of the orchid seed coat viz., smooth periclinal testa walls, strongly raised anticlinal cell wall, average patterns of testa cells forming the longest axis could assist to provide additional information that may be useful in phylogenetic and taxonomic analysis. In all the species undertaken for the current study these set of characters was almost consistent indicating that, they are closely related species showing close affinity as far as their seed characters are concerned.

Adtitti *et al* (1980) studied the patterns of seed growth and suggested that during maturation the seeds elongate as a result of an increase in testa cell length, not number. Therefore, they inferred that increase in percent air space is due to elongation only. This could be one reasons for the more variablity in seed length compared to its counterparts seed width among the *Vanda* species.

Next, the degree of the truncation in seeds was also considered by Arditti *et al* (1980) where length to width ratio of 3.3 in *Cypripedium candidum* was stated to be highly truncated. On the other hand, ratio of 6.25 in *C. acaule* was elongate (calculated from the illustration in Beer, 1863). Basing on this catagorisation, all the seeds of *Vanda* species undertaken in the present work can be said to be relatively truncated although *V. bicolor* seeds stand slightly apart. But more elongated seed cannot be correlated to seed volume whereby width parameter also determines the seed volume.

Patrick *et al* (1980) have agreed that orchid embryos tend to be uniform in size within genera, whereas the dimensions of testa are more variable. Further it was added by Arditti *et al* (1979) that variation in the volumes of embryo is due to length rather than width and deduced that during speciation the seeds of most species become elongated, but their diameter did not increase proportionately. Perhaps this could be the reason why embryo length showed more variation compared to its width in the *Vanda* species.

A light weight is generally given for the great distance traversed by orchid seeds (Close *et al.*, 1978, Went, 1957). Their buoyancy does not seem to have taken into consideration until (Barthlott, 1976) showed that orchid seeds have a high percentage of air space. In addition Burgeff, 1936 & Arditti *et al.*, 1979 pointed out that floatation period in air or increase in flight period may contribute to the distribution of a species. Consequently, seeds with larger seed/embryo volume ratios should be more buoyant than those with smaller ratios. Present investigation in this regard have found that the percentrage air space ranged from 26.51% to 7.01%. As a result, the embryos occupy 73.48% to 92.99% of the seed volume indicating a direct correlation between the volumes of seeds and embryos. However, the *Vanda* species in India could not be correlated to the above statement because maximum air space was found to be in *V. alpina* which has restricted distribution. On the contrary *V. tessellata* and *V. testacea* was found to have lesser percentage of air space compared to *V. alpina* but is found to be distributed more widely extending upto peninsular India. Therefore, the distribution pattern of a species could be more closely related to their nutritional complexities and complementary relationship with the surrounding vegetation and their existence is greatly influenced by their microclimatic conditions and their protective canopy in their habitats as advocated by Vij (1998).

Fig - 6.1

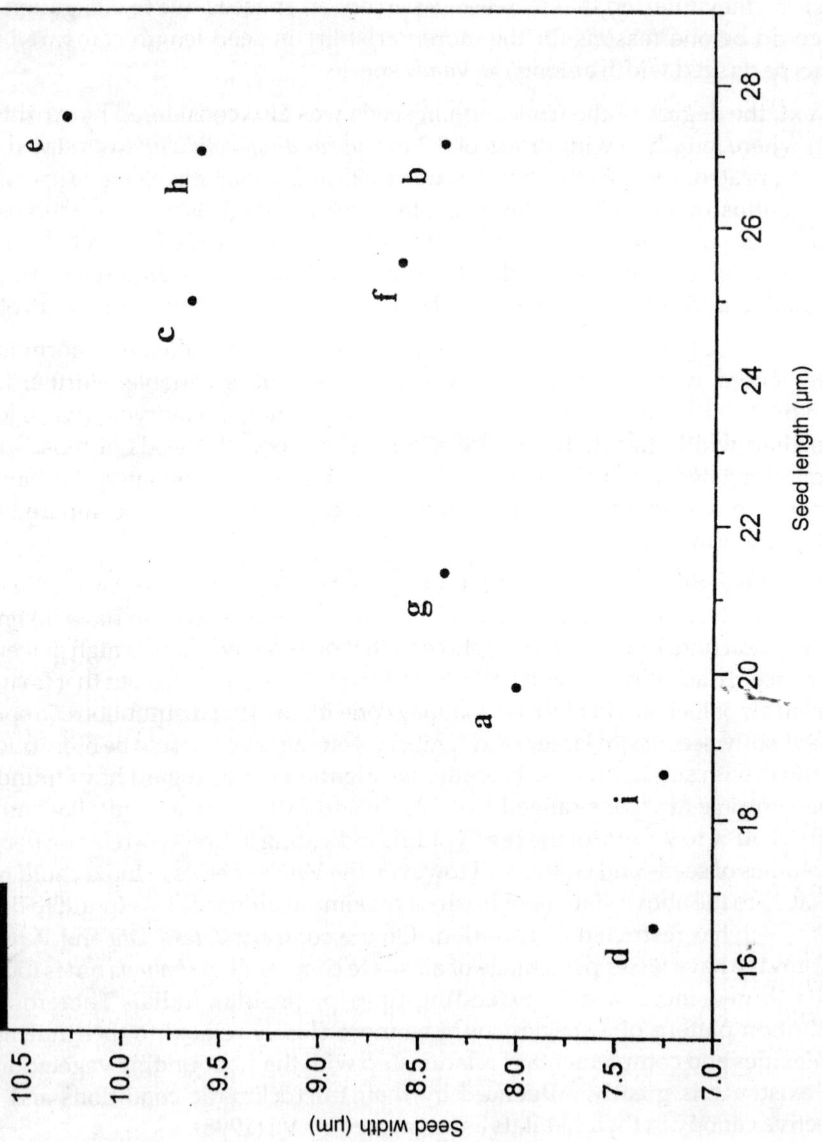


a – *V.alpina*; b – *V.bicolor*; c – *V.coerulea*; d – *V.coerulescens*; e – *V.cristata*; f – *V.liouvillei*; g – *V.stangeana*; h – *V.tessellata*; i – *V.testacea*.

Fig - 6.2

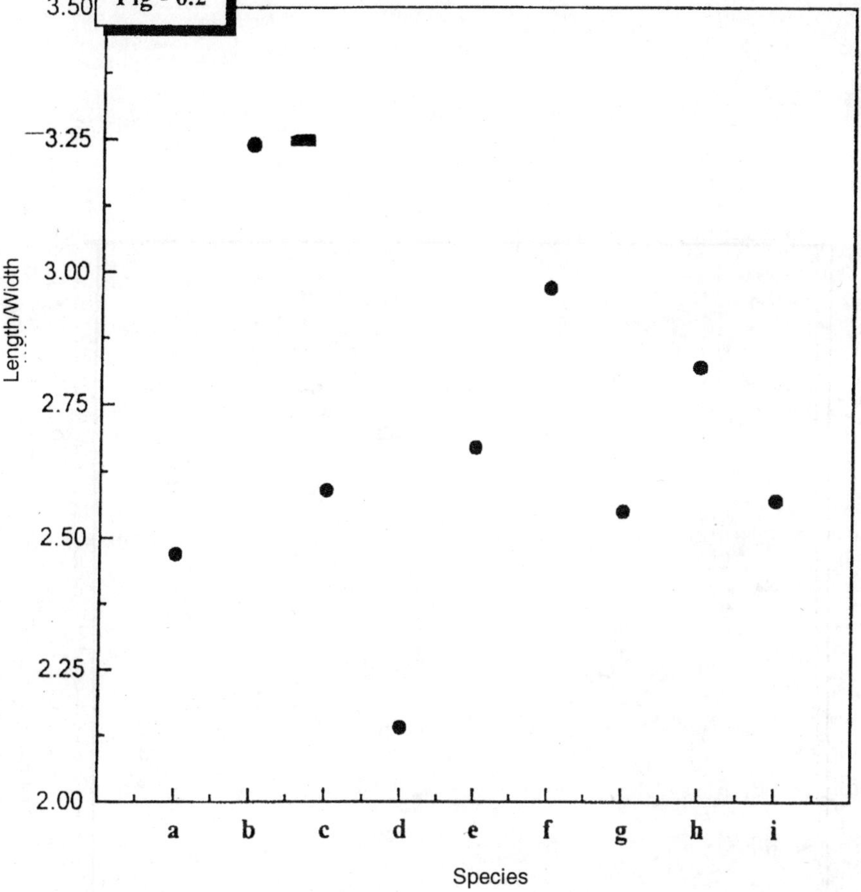


**a** – *V.alpina;* **b** – *V.bicolor,* **c** – *V.coerulea;* **d** – *V.coerulescens;* **e** – *V.cristata;* **f** – *V.liouvillei;* **g** – *V.stangeana;* **h** – *V.tessellata;* **i** – *V.testacea.*

In the species of *Vanda* studied, seed characters appeared to be uniform among the species. For instance, all the species exhibited smooth periclinal testa walls, arrangement of testa cells (Orchis type) and truncated seeds. The Embryos also tend to be relatively uniform among the species. Therefore, the characters considered under the present investigation suggest that the present group *Vanda* represents a closely related species, although their characters are broadly species specific. Thus the information obtained from the study of orchid seed morphometrics are of taxonomic value at generic, tribe and subtribe level. It is also clear that orchid seed morphometry can be brought to bear on several aspects of orchid seed biology.

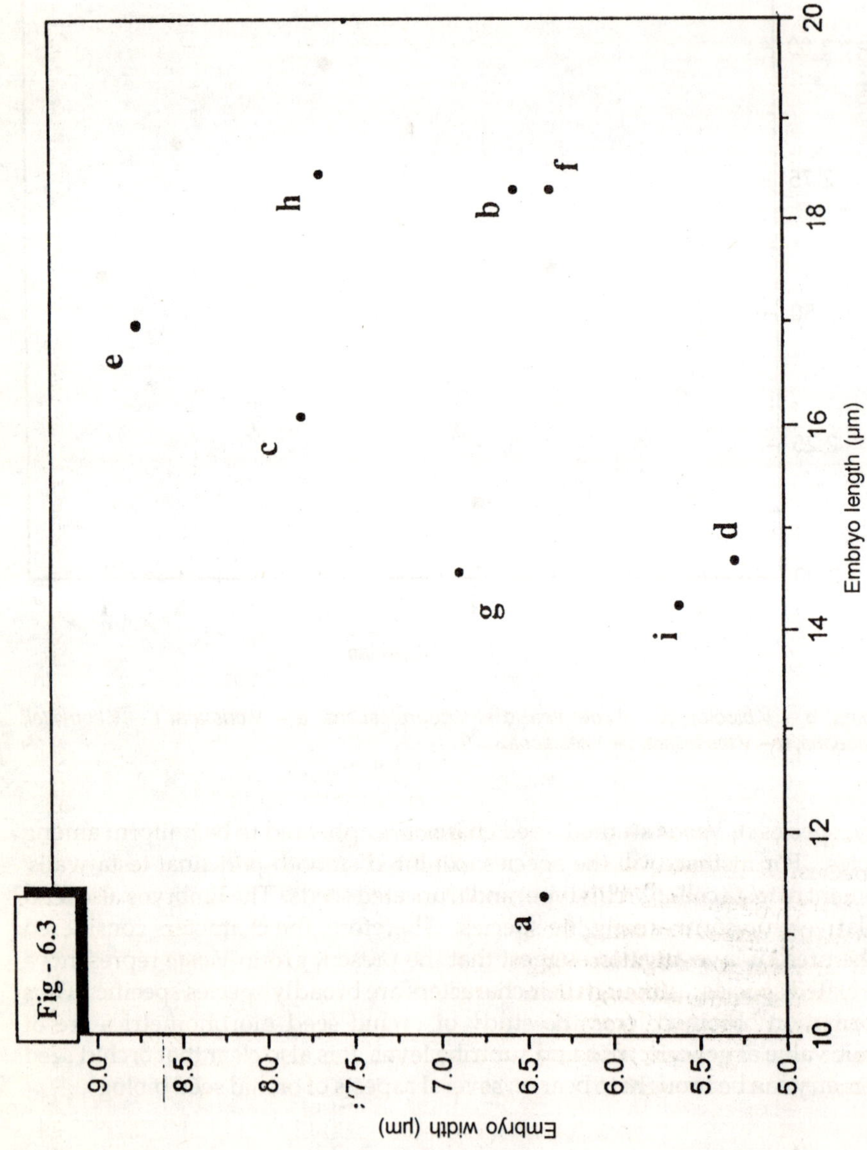


a – *V.alpina*; b – *V.bicolor*, c – *V.coerulea*; d – *V.coerulescens*; e – *V.cristata*; f – *V.liouvillei*; g – *V.stangeana*; h – *V.tessellata*; i – *V.testacea.*

Fig - 6.4

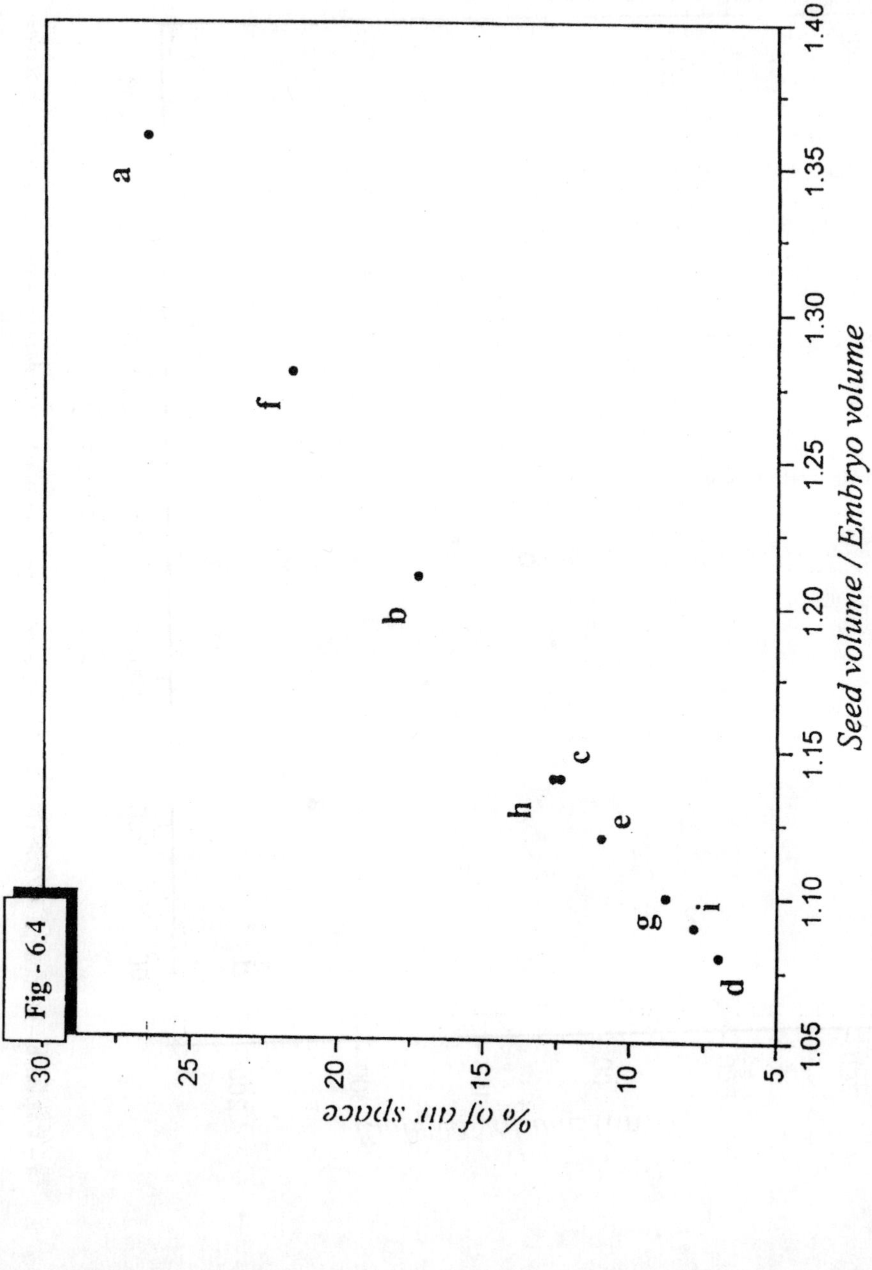


**a** – *V.alpina*; **b** – *V.bicolor*; **c** – *V.coerulea*; **d** – *V.coerulescens*; **e** – *V.cristata*; **f** – *V.liouvillei*; **g** – *V.stangeana*; **h** – *V.tessellata*; **i** – *V.testacea*.

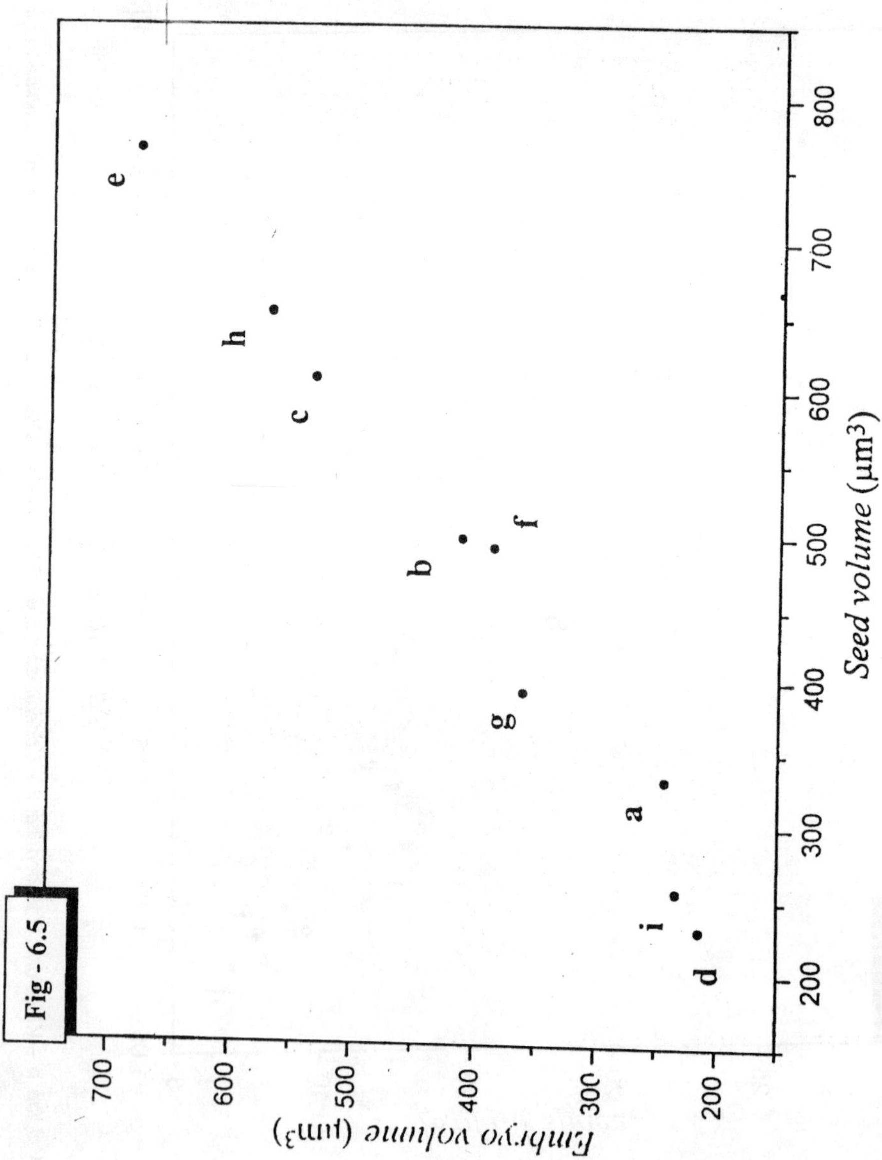


**a** – *V.alpina*; **b** – *V.bicolor*, **c** – *V.coerulea*; **d** – *V.coerulescens*; **e** – *V.cristata*; **f** – *V.liouvillei*; **g** – *V.stangeana*; **h** – *V.tessellata*; **i** – *V.testacea*.

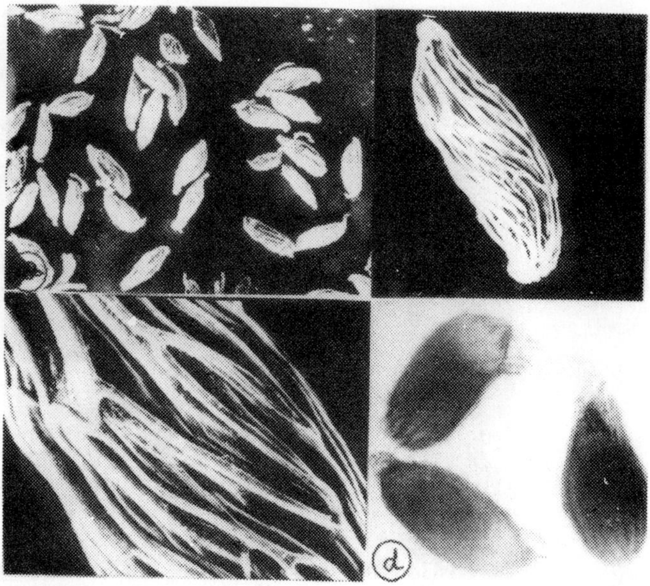

**Plate 6.1:** ***V. alpina***

**SEM**: (a) Group of seeds – **X 60**; (b) Single seed showing arrangement of testa cells – **X 440**; (c) Seed coat magnified – **X 940**;

**LM**: (d) Embryo dimension – **X 16.**

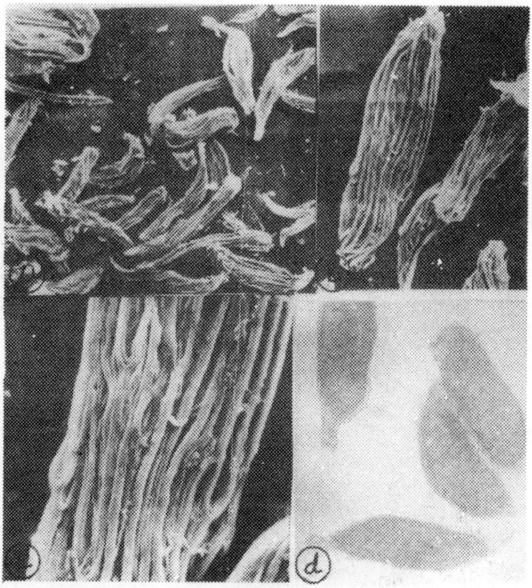

**Plate 6.2:** ***V. bicolor***

**SEM**: (a) Group of seeds – **X 150**; (b) Single seed showing arrangement of testa cells – **X 360**; (c) Seed coat magnified – **X 1000**;

**LM**: (d) Embryo dimension – **X 16.**

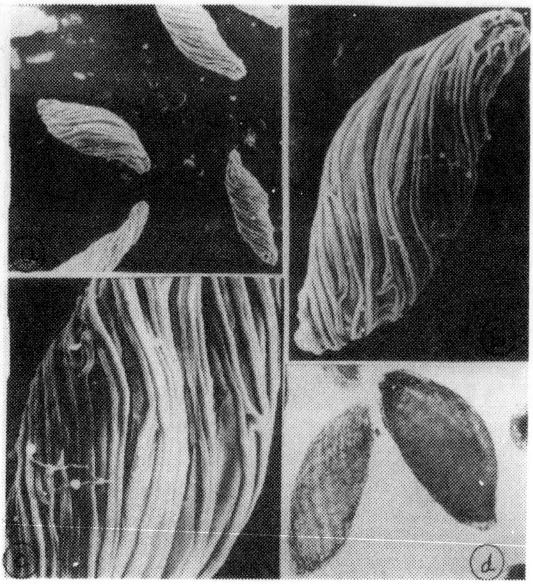


**Plate 6.3:** ***V. coerulea***

**SEM**: (a) Group of seeds – **X 200**; (b) Single seed showing arrangement of testa cells – **X 600**; (c) Seed coat magnified – **X 1000**;

**LM**: (d) Embryo dimension – **X 16.**

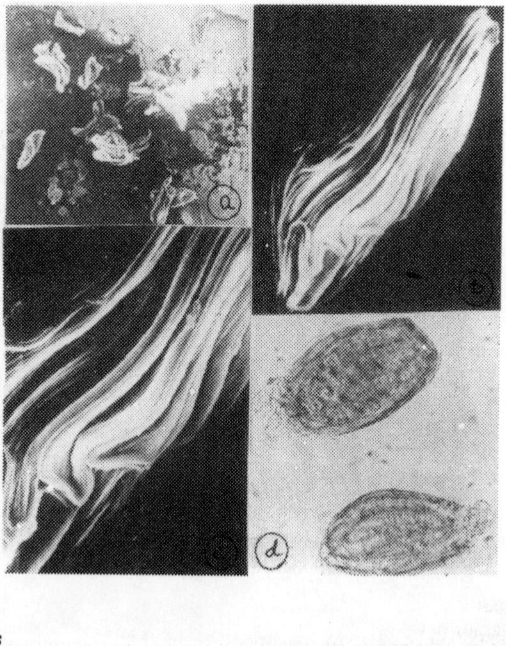


**Plate 6.4:** ***V. coerulescens***

**SEM**: (a) Group of seeds – **X 120**; (b) Single seed showing arrangement of testa cells – **X 860**; (c) Seed coat magnified – **X 1600**;

**LM**: (d) Embryo dimension – **X 16.**

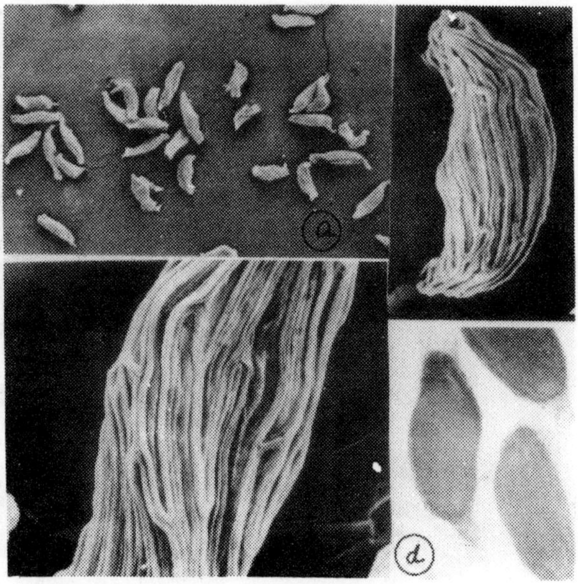

**Plate 6.5:** ***V. cristata***

**SEM**: (a) Group of seeds – **X 60**; (b) Single seed showing arrangement of testa cells – **X 440**; (c) Seed coat magnified – **X 940**;

**LM**: (d) Embryo dimension – **X 16.**

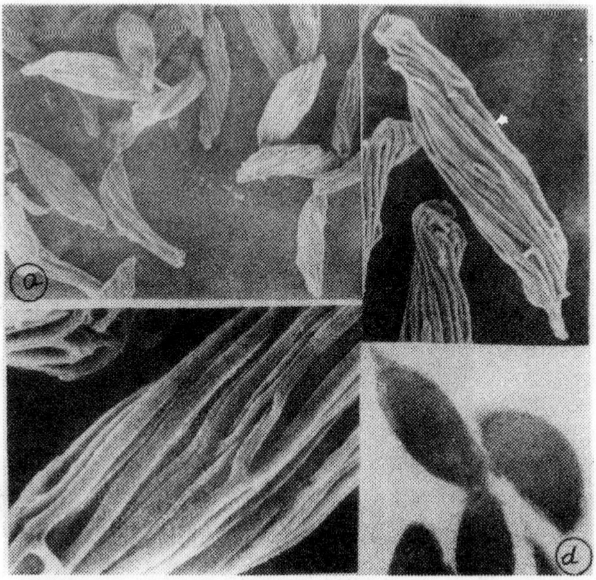

**Plate 6.6:** ***V. liouvillei***

**SEM**: (a) Group of seeds – **X 200**; (b) Single seed showing arrangement of testa cells – **X 450**; (c) Seed coat magnified – **X 1500**;

**LM**: (d) Embryo dimension – **X 16.**

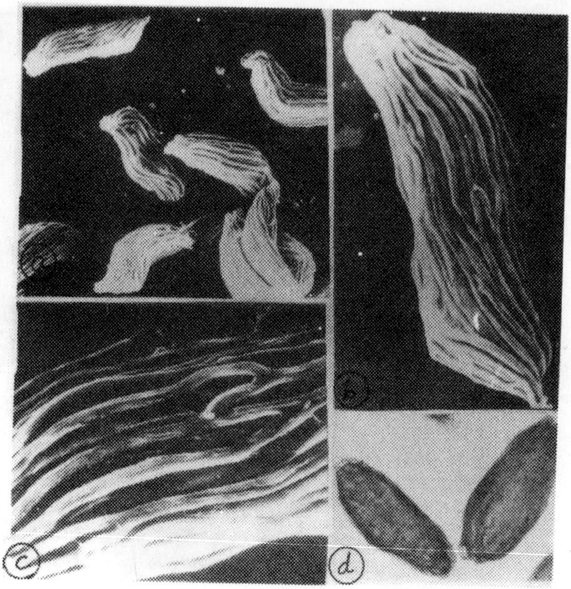

**Plate 6.7:** ***V. stangeana***

**SEM:** (a) Group of seeds – **X 200**; (b) Single seed showing arrangement of testa cells – **X 660**; (c) Seed coat magnified – **X 1300**;

**LM:** (d) Embryo dimension – **X 16.**

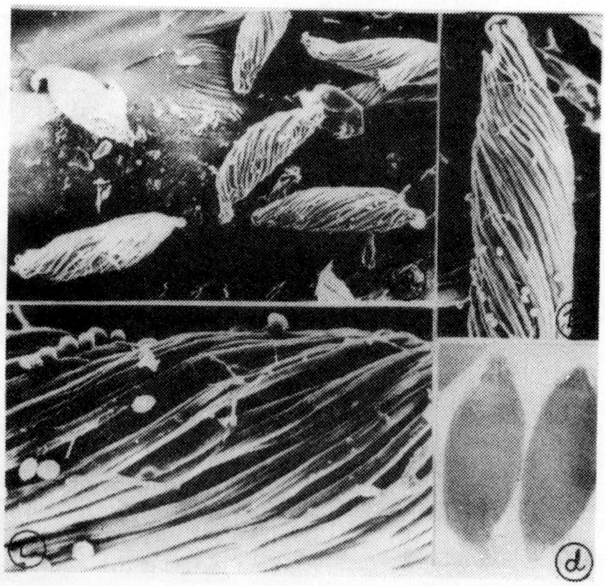

**Plate 6.8:** ***V. tessellata***

**SEM:** (a) Group of seeds – **X 200**; (b) Single seed showing arrangement of testa cells – **X 480**; (c) Seed coat magnified – **X 1200**;

**LM:** (d) Embryo dimension – **X 16.**

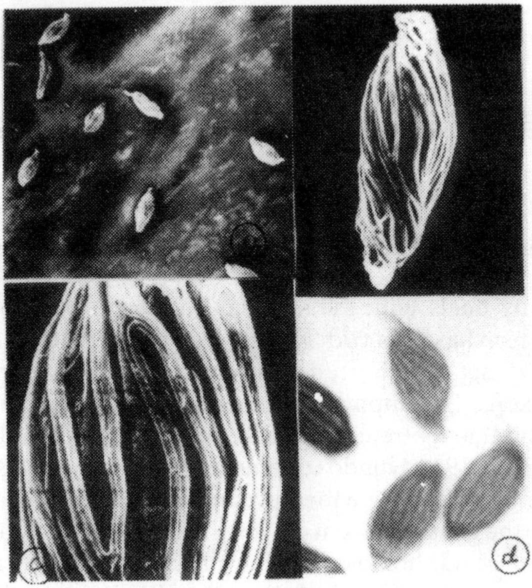

**Plate 6.9: *V. testacea***

**SEM**: (a) Group of seeds – **X 80**; (b) Single seed showing arrangement of testa cells – **X 480**; (c) Seed coat magnified – **X 1300**;

**LM**: (d) Embryo dimension – **X 16.**

# Chapter - 7
# Cytology

Cytotaxonomy deals with the study of number, structure and behaviour of chromosomes which has been widely accepted as a useful tool for the elucidation of taxonomic problems. Such studies help in solving taxonomic problems of controversial taxon. The importance of cytological studies in solving taxonomic problem and evolutionary trend among the orchids has been established by various workers (Kamemoto, 1961; Shindo & Kamemoto, 1963; Sharma & Chatterji, 1966; Vij, 1989). The chromosomes derive their prominence as a tool in taxonomy from their direct relation to the genetic system of which they are an integral part (Lewis, 1957). The study of chromosome homology, number and structure may indicate the extent of relationships and the ways in which the related individuals have evolved (Vij & Shekhar, 1986).

Chromosome number and homology largely determine pairing behaviour at meiosis which in part governs the level of fertility of hybrids and breeding behaviour and patterns of population variation (Stace, 1989). Therefore, the chromosome number determination and analysis of karyotype (the phenotypic appearance of the somatic chromosome) is important in determining relationships between various categories of taxa and also in breeding programmes. Karyotype data can either support taxonomic changes or may suggest otherwise, based on evidences pooled from different sources at all levels of taxonomic hierarchy.

In the classification of orchidaceae, the two major sub divisions of the family, namely, Diandrae and Monandrae, which are primarily based onthe number of stamens, can also undoubtedly be related to chromosome size classes. This has been pointed out by Duncan (1959). It is believed that these two groups separated early in the evolutionary history.

In Indian orchids, the imortant of cytological information has been increasingly realised ever since Sampathkumaram & Seshagiriah (1931) had for the first time brought out cytological features of three Indian orchids taxa. Since then, cytodata of Indian orchids has been gradually accumulating.

There are controversies and confusion in the orchid taxonomy as to the systematic position of some taxa, particularly with a group like sarcanthinae, under which the genus *Vanda* is no exception. This sub-tribe is rather diverse and presents taxonomic complications. The identity of some genera needs thorough analysis based on data combined from different sources, in addition to morphology. Various attempts have been made to trace genome homologies and phylogenetic affinities in this group of orchids using chromosomal features and have variously suggested affinities, segregations and merger of genera and transfer of species (Tanaka and Kamemoto, 1961; Shindo and Kamemoto, 1963b; Sharma and Chatterji, 1966; Arends, 1970; Tara and Kamemoto, 1970; Roy and Sharma, 1972).

A perusal of literature revealed that there seem to be no comprehensive work on the cytological/karyological aspect of Indian *Vandas* except scattered reports on chromosome numbers (Sharma & Chatterji, 1966; Mehra & Vij, 1970; Sau & Sharma, 1983; Vij *et al.*, 1983; Shekar, 1984; Chatterji, 1980). Therefore, the present study is undertaken to present a complete account on the chromosome number and detailed karyotype analysis for the Indian species of *Vanda*.

## Material and Methods

*Root* - tips squash technique was employed for the observation of somatic chromosomes using the following chemical preparation.

1. **Para-dichlorobenzene solution :** A saturated solution of PDB was prepared in distilled water. Pre-treating the root tips with this solution causes contraction and improved the spreading of the chromosomes.
2. **Preparation of Carnoy's fluid :** Added 3 parts of ethyl alcohol with 1 part of glacial acetic acid (3:1 ratio). Sometimes adding 1 part of chloroform was also found to be effective. Carnoy's fluid was used as a fixative to fill the cells rapidly with minimum shrinkage, swelling, distortion and other artifacts.
3. **Preparation of aceto-orcein stain :** 2% aceto-orcein were made by adding 2 gm of orcein powder in 100 ml of 45% acetic acid and heated to dissolve the powder. The solutdion was cooled, filtered and transferred to a glass dropper bottle.

## Procedure

Actively growing root tips were collected and cut longitudinally into four parts for easy penetration of the chemicals and placed in a small borosil bottle containing PDB solution for 3 to 4 hours at 12°-18°C. Then the root sample was washed thoroughly with distilled water and fixed in Carnoy's fluid for about 4 to 6 hours at room temperature. Next, the sample is washed with distilled water for 3-4 times. Then the roots were hydrolysed with 1N Hydrochloric acid at 60°C for 10 to 20 minutes and again washed thoroughly with distilled water. Then the root cap was removed after placing on a clean slide with a drop of 45% acetic acid and spread the cells with the help of a needle. The excess of the acetic acid was blotted out, and 1-2 drops of the stain added and kept for about 20 to 30 minutes. Then covered with a cover clip and tapped thoroughly for spreading the cells as well as the chromosomes. The desired slides were made permanent in Butanol series and mounted in DPX.

The morphology of the chromosomes was observed at metaphase stage of cell division and for chromosome number determination three well spread cells were taken into consideration and recorded at 2n for all the species. For karyotype analysis, microphotographs were taken and enlarged to a magnification of 2000X. The chromosome pair were then cut out and arranged in descending order of lengths placing centromere in one place. From these, data on measurement of chromosomes were taken using 0.5 µm as the unit. Then the actual length were derived by dividing these measurements by the magnification and tabulated.

From the data obtained, r-value (long arm / short arm) for determining type of centromeric chromosome was evaluated. For describing chromosome morphology, terminology of Leavan *et al.* (1964) was adapted; where, m=median centromeric chromosome with arm ratio of 1.0-1.7; sm=sub-median centromeric chromosome with arm ratio of 1.8-3.0; st=sub-terminal centromeric chromosome with arm ratio of 3.1-7.0 and t=terminal centromeric chromosome with arm ratio of 7.1 or more.

For each karyotype, total chromosome length, the mean chromosome length was determined. The S% which is the percentage of the shortest chromosome over the longest chromosome in the karyotype and TF% which is the percentage of the total short arm lengths over the total length of chromosome were calculated using the following formula.

$$S\% = \frac{\text{length of the shortest chromosome}}{\text{length of the longest chromosome}} \times 100$$

$$TF\% = \frac{\text{sum of short arm lengths}}{\text{sum of chromosome lengths}} \times 100$$

The TF% between 50.0 & 30.0 were classed as symmetrical to more or less symmetrical, whereas, those with below 30.0 were class as asymmetrical (Vij & Shekhar, 1986). Therefore, on the basis of TF% the type of karyotype was identified.

## Results and Observations

During the present cytological investigaiton of the Indian species of *Vanda,* the somatic chromosome count from the root tip cells at mitotic metaphase revealed 2n=38 in *V. alpina, V. bicolor,* V.coreulea, *V. cristata, V. liouvillei, V. stangeana, V. tessellata* and *V. testacea* (Plate - 7.1:a,b,c,e & Plate - 7.2:a,c,d,e) while *V. coerulescens* (Plate - 7.1:d) and *V. pumila* (Plate - 7.2:b) revealed 2n=36 and 2n=40 respectively.

Karyotypic studies of different species are illustrated in Plates - 7.3 & 7.4. The following observations were also made with respect to detailes karyotype analysis.

1. *Vanda alpina* : The somatic chromosome count revealed 2n=38. Basing on the r-value the chromosome complement consisted of 22median+12sub-median+4sub-terminal centromeric chromosomes (Table - 7.1). The size of the chromosome ranged from 1 to 3 µm. The total chromosome length was 79.50 (2n) in µm, while the mean chromosome length was 2.09 µm (sd:±0.49). The S% and TF% were 36.36 and 39.62 respectively (Table - 7.11).
2. *Vanda bicolor* : The somatic chromosome count revealed 2n=38. Basing on the r-value the chromosome complement consisted of 30median+8sub-median centromeric chromosomes (Table - 7.2). The size of the chromosome ranged from 1.75 to 3 µm. The total chromosome length was 88.50 (2n) in µm, while the mean chromosome length was 2.33 µm (sd:±0.40). The S% and TF% were 58.33 and 35.03 respectively (Table - 7.11).

3. *Vanda coerulea* : The somatic chromosome count revealed 2n=38. Basing on the r-value the chromosome complement consisted of 26median+4sub-median+8sub-terminal centromeric chromosomes (Table - 7.3). The size of the chromosome ranged from 1 to 3 µm. The total chromosome length was 82.00 (2n) in µm, while the mean chromosome length was 2.16 µm (sd:±0.52). The S% and TF% were 33.33 and 33.54 respectively (Table - 7.11).
4. *Vanda coerulescens* : The somatic chromosome count revealed 2n=36. Basing on the r-value the chromosome complement consisted of 18median+8sub-median+10sub-terminal centromeric chromosomes (Table - 7.4). The size of the chromosome ranged from 1 to 2.55 µm . The total chromosome length was 65.00 (2n) in µm, while the mean chromosome length was 1.81 µm (sd:±0.34). The S% and TF% were 44.44 and 32.31 respectively (Table - 7.11).
5. *Vanda cristata* : The somatic chromosome count revealed 2n=38. Basing on the r-value the chromosome complement consisted of 24median+6sub-median+8sub-terminal centromeric chromosomes (Table - 7.5). The size of the chromosome ranged from 1.25 to 2.5 µm. The total chromosome length was 76.50 (2n) in µm, while the mean chromosome length was 2.01 µm (sd:±0.36). The S% and TF% were 50.00 and 32.03 respectively (Table - 7.11).
6. *Vanda liouvillei* : The somatic chromosome count revealed 2n=38. Basing on the r-value the chromosome complement consisted of 26median+8sub-median+4sub-terminal centromeric chromosomes (Table - 7.6). The size of the chromosome ranged from 1 to 3 µm. The total chromosome length was 74.00 (2n) in µm, while the mean chromosome length was 1.95 µm (sd:±0.46). The S% and TF% were 33.33 and 38.51 respectively (Table - 7.11).
7. *Vanda pumila* : The somatic chromosome count revealed 2n=40. Basing on the r-value the chromosome complement consisted of 24median+4sub-median+6sub-terminal centromeric chromosomes (Table - 7.7). The size of the chromosome ranged from 1 to 3 µm. The total chromosome length was 86.50 (2n) in µm, while the mean chromosome length was 2.16 µm (sd:±0.63). The S% and TF% were 33.33 and 38.15 respectively (Table - 7.11).
8. *Vanda stangeana* : The somatic chromosome count revealed 2n=38. Basing on the r-value the chromosome complement consisted of 28median+8sub-median+2sub-terminal centromeric chromosomes (Table - 7.8). The size of the chromosome ranged from 1.25 to 3 µm. The total chromosome length was 84.50 (2n) in µm, while the mean chromosome length was 2.22 µm (sd:±0.56). The S% and TF% were 41.67 and 38.46 respectively (Table - 7.11).
9. *Vanda tessellata* : The somatic chromosome count revealed 2n=38. Basing on the r-value the chromosome complement consisted of 22median+2sub-median+14sub-terminal centromeric chromosomes (Table - 7.9). The size of the chromosome ranged from 1 to 2.75 µm. The total chromosome length was 77.00 (2n) in µm, while the mean chromosome length was 2.03 µm (sd:±0.56). The S% and TF% were 36.36 and 35.71 respectively (Table - 7.11).
10. *Vanda testacea* : The somatic chromosome count revealed 2n=38. Basing on the r-value the chromosome complement consisted of 30median+8sub-median

centromeric chromosomes (Table - 7.10). The size of the chromosome ranged from 1.25 to 3 µm. The total chromosome length was 88.00 (2n) in µm, while the mean chromosome length was 2.41 µm (sd:±0.56). The S% and TF% were 41.67 and 38.64 respectively (Table - 7.11).

## Discussion

Somatic chromosome number of 2n=38 in the case of *V. bicolor* is investigated cytologically for the first time and reported here, because the species is less known and rarely mentioned in literature. Another new report has been made for *V. liouvillei* as 2n-38. This species was also poorly knwon and has not been mentioned in the literature since its original publication by Finet (1913) and later by Seidenfaden (1988) and Phukan (1995). Somatic chromosome number of 2n-38 in *V. alpina* confirms earlier identical reports (Mehra & Vij, 1970; Sau & Sharma, 1983). In *V. coerulea* the present study revealed 2n-38 chromosomes which is in conformation to the earlier reports (Sharma & Chatterji, 1966; Vij *et al.*, 1983; Mehra & Shegal, 1980; Shekhar, 1984; Chatterji, 1990). There is also a record that a variation nucleus with 2n=36 chromosomes in *V. coerulea* by Sharma & Chatterji (1966); however, during the present study we have not encountered the occurrence of this variation, *V. coerulescens* revealed 2n=36 from the somatic chromosome count. However, previous reports showed 2n=38 (Sharma & Chatterji, 1966; Chatterji, 1990). While Sau & Sharam (1983) reported 2n=40 chromosomes. In *V. cristata* 2n=38 was noted in the present study which agreed with the earlier reports (Mehra & Kashyap, 1976; Sharma & Chatterji, 1966; Vij *et al*, 1983). Besides, 2n=76 was also reported by Mehra & Kashyap, (1984d) but during the present study this number has not been observed in *V. cristata*. In *V. pumila* the present count revealed 2n=40 which support the sole report made by Sau & Sharma (1983). Present findings in *V. stangeana* as 2n=38 is also in accord with the previous two reports (Vij *et al.*, 1983; Hegde & Ingalhalli, 1985). V. tesellata with 2n=38 in the present count agrees with the the reports made by Sharma & Chatterji (1960, 1966), Sau & Sharma (1983), Abraham & Vatsala (1981), Chatterji (1990). Although somatic chromosome variation was reported by Sharma & Chatterji (1966), present investigation has not encountered this variation in the somatic cells. *V. testacea* also revealed 2n=38 chromosomes which supports the earlier findings by Vij *et al* (1981), Sau & Sharma (1983).

Of the 10*Vanda* species investigated, 8 species revealed 2n=38 somatic chromosomes while 2 species revealed 2n=36 and 2n=40 respectively. Sau & Sharma (1983) are of the opinion that in the genus *Vanda* 2n=19 is certainly a deep seated number which is present in species inhabiting different climatic regions. However, the genus also shows chromosomal races in several species (Chardard, 1963; Sharma & Chatterji, 1966).

Detailed karyotype analysis showed that the total chromosome length varied among the species. The smallest chromosome set was that of *V. coerulescens* and the largest chromosome set was that of *V. bicolor*. The difference between these two karyotypes was 23.00 µm which can account for their specific status and also reflect their primitive and advanced feature among the *Vanda* species. On the other hand, the difference between the mean chromosome lengths among the species was only 0.6 µm suggesting thereby that they are closely related species.

The S% which gives an idea about the variation in chromosome length range from 33.33% to 58.33%. The higher value indicate more uniformity while the lower value suggest the degree of variation in the karyotype. Besides, the range of chrmosome length among the species was from 1 to 3 µm which can be said a medium to short chromosomes. The chromosomes were mostly median to sub-median and a few sub-terminal centromeric chromosomes. In the evolutionary hierarchy, a karyotype of median centromere is generally considered as an ancestral condition from which other centromeric locations are derived. However, according to Chatterji (1986) the situation in orchid seems to be confusing. Highly evolved subtribes like Cymbidiinae and Sarcanthinae posses median to submedian chromosomes. Hence, the karyotype pattern may indicate several cycles of symmetry and asymmetry during speciation in orchids.

An estimate of the mean position of centromere in different chromosomes is reflected by the TF%. It ranged between 32.02 and 38.64 which falls under the class of symmetrical karyotype. It is evident that both the centromere position and chromosome length has enchanced the karyotype symmetry in the *Vanda* species investigated.

The genus *Vanda* show a numerical consistency of chromosome number 2n=38 with occasional deviation in *V. coerulescens* 2n=36 and 2n=40 in *V. pumila*. Present study supports separation of terete leaved species (*V. teres*) from *Vanda* to *Paplionanthe teres* having comparatively larger chromosome and asymmetrical karyotype (Schlecter, 1926; Holttum, 1959; Chatterji, 1986; Vij, 1989), whereas true *Vanda* species posses small chrmosomes with symmetrical karyotypes as observed in present study. According to Chatterji (1986) large chromosomes, low basic set (x = 10,12,13) in the karyotype are suggestive of homogeneity and primitiveness of Diandrae. On the other hand, Monandrae with medium to short chromosomes, diverse basic sets (x=19,20 being deep-seated) in the chromosome complements shows characteristic of advance features.

Presnet cytological investigation in the genus *Vanda* indicate that, karyotype details do not vary significantly in all its species despite the variation in the total length of chromosome content. Thus, present cytological studies do not support transfer of *V. alpina*, *V. cristata* and *V. pumila* to a new genus *Trudelia* (Garey, 1986). However, minute alterations have been effective factors in evolution according to Sau & Sharma (1983). Hence the genus constitute a homogenous assemblages from the cytological point of view and the differences in individual karyotype have played a role in the evolution of species.

The small size chromosomes have favoured and contributed to the rich infra specific biodiversity which has been dealt else where (Chapter - 2 : Biodiversity) in the present study. It appears that while maintaining the constancy in the number of chromosomes in this group, speciation has occured through gene mutation and/or structural rearrangement in the chromosomes. The structural changes and gene mutation has been reported as most prevalent mode of speciation in 72.25% of the investigated Indian orchids (Vij, 1989).

**Table - 7.1 : *V. alpina* (Chromosome morphology).**

| Chromosome pair (2n) | Chromosome length (μm) | | | r-value la/sa | Type of chromosome |
|---|---|---|---|---|---|
| | Total | long arm (la) | short arm (sa) | | |
| 1 | 2.75 | 1.50 | 1.25 | 1.50 | m |
| 2 | 2.75 | 1.50 | 1.25 | 1.50 | m |
| 3 | 2.50 | 1.25 | 1.00 | 1.25 | m |
| 4 | 2.50 | 1.25 | 1.00 | 1.25 | m |
| 5 | 2.50 | 1.25 | 1.00 | 1.25 | m |
| 6 | 2.50 | 1.50 | 0.75 | 2.00 | sm |
| 7 | 2.50 | 1.50 | 0.75 | 2.00 | sm |
| 8 | 2.25 | 1.00 | 1.00 | 1.00 | m |
| 9 | 2.25 | 1.00 | 1.00 | 1.00 | m |
| 10 | 2.25 | 1.00 | 1.00 | 1.00 | m |
| 11 | 2.00 | 1.00 | 0.75 | 1.33 | m |
| 12 | 2.00 | 1.00 | 0.75 | 1.33 | m |
| 13 | 2.00 | 1.00 | 0.75 | 1.33 | m |
| 14 | 1.75 | 1.00 | 0.50 | 2.00 | sm |
| 15 | 1.75 | 1.00 | 0.50 | 2.00 | sm |
| 16 | 1.50 | 1.00 | 0.25 | 4.00 | st |
| 17 | 1.50 | 1.00 | 0.25 | 4.00 | st |
| 18 | 1.25 | 0.75 | 0.25 | 3.00 | sm |
| 19 | 1.00 | 0.50 | 0.25 | 2.00 | sm |

**Table - 7.2 : *V. bicolor* (Chromosome morphology).**

| Chromosome pair (2n) | Chromosome length (μm) | | | r-value la/sa | Type of chromosome |
|---|---|---|---|---|---|
| | Total | long arm (la) | short arm (sa) | | |
| 1 | 3.00 | 1.50 | 1.25 | 1.20 | m |
| 2 | 3.00 | 1.50 | 1.25 | 1.20 | m |
| 3 | 2.75 | 1.50 | 1.00 | 1.50 | m |
| 4 | 2.75 | 1.50 | 1.00 | 1.50 | m |
| 5 | 2.75 | 1.50 | 1.00 | 1.50 | m |
| 6 | 2.50 | 1.25 | 1.00 | 1.25 | m |
| 7 | 2.50 | 1.25 | 1.00 | 1.25 | m |
| 8 | 2.50 | 1.25 | 1.00 | 1.25 | m |
| 9 | 2.25 | 1.00 | 1.00 | 1.00 | m |
| 10 | 2.25 | 1.00 | 1.00 | 1.00 | m |
| 11 | 2.25 | 1.25 | 0.75 | 1.67 | m |
| 12 | 2.25 | 1.25 | 0.75 | 1.67 | m |
| 13 | 2.52 | 1.25 | 0.75 | 1.67 | m |
| 14 | 2.00 | 1.00 | 0.75 | 1.33 | m |
| 15 | 2.00 | 1.00 | 0.75 | 1.33 | m |
| 16 | 2.00 | 1.25 | 0.50 | 1.50 | sm |
| 17 | 1.75 | 1.25 | 0.25 | 5.00 | sm |
| 18 | 1.75 | 1.25 | 0.25 | 5.00 | sm |
| 19 | 1.75 | 1.25 | 0.25 | 5.00 | sm |

**Table - 7.3 : *V. coerulea* (Chromosome morphology).**

| *Chromosome pair (2n)* | *Chromosome length (μm)* | | | *r-value la/sa* | *Type of chromosome* |
|---|---|---|---|---|---|
| | *Total* | *long arm (la)* | *short arm (sa)* | | |
| 1 | 3.00 | 1.50 | 1.25 | 1.20 | m |
| 2 | 2.75 | 1.25 | 1.25 | 1.00 | m |
| 3 | 2.75 | 1.25 | 1.25 | 1.00 | m |
| 4 | 2.75 | 1.25 | 1.25 | 1.00 | m |
| 5 | 2.50 | 1.25 | 1.00 | 1.25 | m |
| 6 | 2.50 | 1.25 | 1.00 | 1.25 | m |
| 7 | 2.50 | 1.25 | 1.00 | 1.25 | m |
| 8 | 2.50 | 1.50 | 0.75 | 2.00 | sm |
| 9 | 2.25 | 1.25 | 0.75 | 1.67 | m |
| 10 | 2.00 | 1.00 | 0.745 | 1.67 | m |
| 11 | 2.00 | 1.00 | 0.745 | 1.67 | m |
| 12 | 2.00 | 1.25 | 0.50 | 2. 50 | m |
| 13 | 2.00 | 1.25 | 0.50 | 2. 50 | m |
| 14 | 2.00 | 1.25 | 0.50 | 2. 50 | m |
| 15 | 1.75 | 1.25 | 0.25 | 5.00 | st |
| 16 | 1.75 | 1.25 | 0.25 | 5.00 | st |
| 17 | 1.50 | 1.00 | 0.25 | 4.00 | st |
| 18 | 1.50 | 1.00 | 0.25 | 4.00 | st |
| 19 | 1.00 | 0.50 | 0.25 | 2.00 | sm |

**Table - 7.4 : *V. coerulescens* (Chromosome morphology).**

| *Chromosome pair (2n)* | *Chromosome length (μm)* | | | *r-value la/sa* | *Type of chromosome* |
|---|---|---|---|---|---|
| | *Total* | *long arm (la)* | *short arm (sa)* | | |
| 1 | 2.25 | 1.00 | 1.00 | 1.00 | m |
| 2 | 2.25 | 1.00 | 1.00 | 1.00 | m |
| 3 | 2.25 | 1.00 | 1.00 | 1.00 | m |
| 4 | 2.00 | 1.00 | 0.75 | 1.33 | m |
| 5 | 2.00 | 1.00 | 0.75 | 1.33 | m |
| 6 | 2.00 | 1.00 | 0.75 | 1.33 | m |
| 7 | 2.00 | 1.00 | 0.75 | 1.33 | m |
| 8 | 2.00 | 1.00 | 0.75 | 1.33 | m |
| 9 | 2.00 | 1.00 | 0.75 | 1.33 | m |
| 10 | 1.75 | 1.00 | 0.50 | 2.00 | sm |
| 11 | 1.75 | 1.00 | 0.50 | 2.00 | sm |
| 12 | 1.75 | 1.00 | 0.50 | 2.00 | sm |
| 13 | 1.50 | 1.00 | 0.25 | 4.00 | st |
| 14 | 1.50 | 1.00 | 0.25 | 4.00 | st |
| 15 | 1.50 | 1.00 | 0.25 | 4.00 | st |
| 16 | 1.50 | 1.00 | 0.25 | 4.00 | st |
| 17 | 1.50 | 1.00 | 0.25 | 4.00 | st |
| 18 | 1.00 | 0.50 | 0.25 | 2.00 | sm |

**Table - 7.5 : *V. cristata* (Chromosome morphology).**

| *Chromosome pair (2n)* | *Chromosome length (µm)* | | | *r-value la/sa* | *Type of chromosome* |
|---|---|---|---|---|---|
| | *Total* | *long arm (la)* | *short arm (sa)* | | |
| 1 | 2.50 | 1.25 | 1.00 | 1.25 | m |
| 2 | 2.50 | 1.25 | 1.00 | 1.25 | m |
| 3 | 2.50 | 1.25 | 1.00 | 1.25 | m |
| 4 | 2.25 | 1.25 | 0.75 | 1.67 | m |
| 5 | 2.25 | 1.25 | 0.75 | 1.67 | m |
| 6 | 2.25 | 1.25 | 0.75 | 1.67 | m |
| 7 | 2.25 | 1.25 | 0.75 | 1.67 | m |
| 8 | 2.25 | 1.25 | 0.75 | 1.67 | m |
| 9 | 2.25 | 1.25 | 0.75 | 1.67 | m |
| 10 | 2.00 | 1.00 | 0.75 | 1.33 | m |
| 11 | 2.00 | 1.00 | 0.75 | 1.33 | m |
| 12 | 2.00 | 1.00 | 0.75 | 1.33 | m |
| 13 | 1.75 | 1.00 | 0.50 | 2.00 | sm |
| 14 | 1.75 | 1.00 | 0.50 | 2.00 | sm |
| 15 | 1.75 | 1.00 | 0.50 | 2.00 | sm |
| 16 | 1.50 | 1.00 | 0.25 | 4.00 | st |
| 17 | 1.50 | 1.00 | 0.25 | 4.00 | st |
| 18 | 1.25 | 0.75 | 0.25 | 3.00 | sm |
| 19 | 1.25 | 0.75 | 0.25 | 3.00 | sm |

**Table - 7.6 : *V. liouvillei* (Chromosome morphology).**

| *Chromosome pair (2n)* | *Chromosome iength (µm)* | | | *r-value la/sa* | *Type of chromosome* |
|---|---|---|---|---|---|
| | *Total* | *long arm (la)* | *short arm (sa)* | | |
| 1 | 3.00 | 1.50 | 1.25 | 1.20 | m |
| 2 | 3.00 | 1.50 | 1.25 | 1.20 | m |
| 3 | 2.50 | 1.25 | 1.00 | 1.25 | m |
| 4 | 2.50 | 1.25 | 1.00 | 1.25 | m |
| 5 | 2.50 | 1.25 | 1.00 | 1.25 | m |
| 6 | 2.50 | 1.25 | 1.00 | 1.25 | m |
| 7 | 2.50 | 1.25 | 1.00 | 1.25 | m |
| 8 | 2.25 | 1.00 | 1.00 | 1.00 | m |
| 9 | 2.00 | 1.00 | 0.75 | 1.33 | m |
| 10 | 2.00 | 1.00 | 0.75 | 1.33 | m |
| 11 | 2.00 | 1.00 | 0.75 | 1.33 | m |
| 12 | 2.00 | 1.00 | 0.75 | 1.33 | m |
| 13 | 2.00 | 1.00 | 0.75 | 1.33 | m |
| 14 | 1.75 | 1.00 | 0.50 | 2.00 | sm |
| 15 | 1.75 | 1.00 | 0.50 | 2.00 | sm |
| 16 | 1.50 | 1.00 | 0.25 | 4.00 | st |
| 17 | 1.50 | 1.00 | 0.25 | 4.00 | st |
| 18 | 1.25 | 0.75 | 0.25 | 3.00 | sm |
| 19 | 1.00 | 0.50 | 0.25 | 2.00 | sm |

**Table - 7.7 : *V. pumila* (Chromosome morphology).**

| Chromosome pair (2n) | Chromosome length (μm) | | | r-value la/sa | Type of chromosome |
|---|---|---|---|---|---|
| | Total | long arm (la) | short arm (sa) | | |
| 1 | 3.00 | 1.50 | 1.25 | 1.20 | m |
| 2 | 3.00 | 1.50 | 1.25 | 1.20 | m |
| 3 | 3.00 | 1.50 | 1.25 | 1.20 | m |
| 4 | 2.75 | 1.25 | 1.25 | 1.00 | m |
| 5 | 2.75 | 1.25 | 1.25 | 1.00 | m |
| 6 | 2.50 | 1.25 | 1.00 | 1.25 | m |
| 7 | 2.50 | 1.25 | 1.00 | 1.25 | m |
| 8 | 2.50 | 1.25 | 1.00 | 1.25 | m |
| 9 | 2.25 | 1.00 | 1.00 | 1.00 | m |
| 10 | 2.25 | 1.00 | 1.00 | 1.00 | m |
| 11 | 2.25 | 1.00 | 1.00 | 1.00 | m |
| 12 | 2.25 | 1.00 | 1.00 | 1.00 | m |
| 13 | 2.25 | 1.00 | 1.00 | 1.00 | m |
| 14 | 2.00 | 1.00 | 0.75 | 1.33 | m |
| 15 | 1.50 | 1.00 | 0.25 | 4.00 | st |
| 16 | 1.50 | 1.00 | 0.25 | 4.00 | st |
| 17 | 1.50 | 1.00 | 0.25 | 4.00 | st |
| 18 | 1.25 | 0.75 | 0.25 | 3.00 | sm |
| 19 | 1.25 | 0.75 | 0.25 | 3.00 | sm |
| 20 | 1.00 | 0.50 | 0.25 | 2.00 | sm |

**Table - 7.8 : *V. stangeana* (Chromosome morphology).**

| Chromosome pair (2n) | Chromosome length (μm) | | | r-value la/sa | Type of chromosome |
|---|---|---|---|---|---|
| | Total | long arm (la) | short arm (sa) | | |
| 1 | 3.00 | 1.50 | 1.25 | 1.20 | m |
| 2 | 3.00 | 1.50 | 1.25 | 1.20 | m |
| 3 | 3.00 | 1.50 | 1.25 | 1.20 | m |
| 4 | 2.75 | 1.25 | 1.25 | 1.00 | m |
| 5 | 2.75 | 1.25 | 1.25 | 1.00 | m |
| 6 | 2.50 | 1.25 | 1.00 | 1.25 | m |
| 7 | 2.50 | 1.25 | 1.00 | 1.25 | m |
| 8 | 2.50 | 1.25 | 1.00 | 1.25 | m |
| 9 | 2.25 | 1.00 | 1.00 | 1.00 | m |
| 10 | 2.25 | 1.00 | 1.00 | 1.00 | m |
| 11 | 2.25 | 1.00 | 1.00 | 1.00 | m |
| 12 | 2.00 | 1.00 | 0.75 | 1.33 | m |
| 13 | 2.00 | 1.00 | 0.75 | 1.33 | m |
| 14 | 2.00 | 1.00 | 0.75 | 1.33 | m |
| 15 | 1.75 | 1.00 | 0.50 | 2.00 | sm |
| 16 | 1.75 | 1.00 | 0.50 | 2.00 | sm |
| 17 | 1.50 | 1.00 | 0.25 | 4.00 | st |
| 18 | 1.25 | 0.75 | 0.25 | 3.00 | sm |
| 19 | 1.25 | 0.75 | 0.25 | 3.00 | sm |

**Table - 7.9 : *V. tessellata* (Chromosome morphology).**

| *Chromosome pair (2n)* | *Chromosome length (μm)* | | | *r-value la/sa* | *Type of chromosome* |
|---|---|---|---|---|---|
| | *Total* | *long arm (la)* | *short arm (sa)* | | |
| 1 | 2.75 | 1.25 | 1.25 | 1.00 | m |
| 2 | 2.75 | 1.25 | 1.25 | 1.00 | m |
| 3 | 2.75 | 1.25 | 1.25 | 1.00 | m |
| 4 | 2.75 | 1.25 | 1.25 | 1.00 | m |
| 5 | 2.50 | 1.25 | 1.00 | 1.25 | m |
| 6 | 2.50 | 1.25 | 1.00 | 1.25 | m |
| 7 | 2.25 | 1.00 | 1.00 | 1.00 | m |
| 8 | 2.25 | 1.00 | 1.00 | 1.00 | m |
| 9 | 2.25 | 1.00 | 1.00 | 1.00 | m |
| 10 | 2.25 | 1.00 | 1.00 | 1.00 | m |
| 11 | 2.00 | 1.00 | 0.75 | 1.33 | m |
| 12 | 1.50 | 1.0 | 0.25 | 4.00 | st |
| 13 | 1.50 | 1.0 | 0.25 | 4.00 | st |
| 14 | 1.50 | 1.0 | 0.25 | 4.00 | st |
| 15 | 1.50 | 1.0 | 0.25 | 4.00 | st |
| 16 | 1.50 | 1.0 | 0.25 | 4.00 | st |
| 17 | 1.50 | 1.0 | 0.25 | 4.00 | st |
| 18 | 1.50 | 1.0 | 0.25 | 4.00 | st |
| 19 | 1.00 | 0.50 | 0.25 | 2.00 | sm |

**Table - 7.10 : *V. testaceae* (Chromosome morphology).**

| *Chromosome pair (2n)* | *Chromosome length (μm)* | | | *r-value la/sa* | *Type of chromosome* |
|---|---|---|---|---|---|
| | *Total* | *long arm (la)* | *short arm (sa)* | | |
| 1 | 3.00 | 1.50 | 1.00 | 1.50 | m |
| 2 | 3.00 | 1.50 | 1.00 | 1.50 | m |
| 3 | 2.75 | 1.50 | 1.00 | 1.50 | m |
| 4 | 2.75 | 1.50 | 1.00 | 1.50 | m |
| 5 | 2.75 | 1.50 | 1.00 | 1.50 | m |
| 6 | 2.75 | 1.25 | 1.25 | 1.00 | m |
| 7 | 2.75 | 1.25 | 1.25 | 1.00 | m |
| 8 | 2.50 | 1.25 | 1.00 | 1.25 | m |
| 9 | 2.50 | 1.25 | 1.00 | 1.25 | m |
| 10 | 2.50 | 1.25 | 1.00 | 1.25 | m |
| 11 | 2.25 | 1.00 | 1.00 | 1.00 | m |
| 12 | 2.25 | 1.00 | 1.00 | 1.00 | m |
| 13 | 2.25 | 1.00 | 1.00 | 1.00 | m |
| 14 | 2.00 | 1.00 | 0.75 | 1.33 | m |
| 15 | 2.00 | 1.00 | 0.75 | 1.33 | m |
| 16 | 1.75 | 1.00 | 0.50 | 2.00 | m |
| 17 | 1.75 | 1.00 | 0.50 | 2.00 | sm |
| 18 | 1.25 | 0.75 | 0.25 | 3.00 | sm |
| 19 | 1.25 | 0.75 | 0.25 | 3.00 | sm |

**Table - 7.11 : Karyotype analysis of *Vanda* species.**

| *Species* | *Chromosome number (2n)* | *Total Chromosome length (2n) in μm* | *Mean Chromosome length in μm/sd* | *S%* | *TF%* | *Karyotype formula* |
|---|---|---|---|---|---|---|
| *V. alpina* | 38 | 79.50 | 2.08/0.49 | 36.36 | 39.62 | 22m+12sm+4st |
| *V. bicolor* | 38 | 8.50 | 2.33/0.40 | 58.33 | 35.03 | 30m+8sm |
| *V. coerulea* | 38 | 82.00 | 2.16/0.52 | 33.33 | 33.54 | 26m+4sm+8st |
| *V. coerulescens* | 36 | 65.00 | 1.81/0.34 | 44.44 | 32.31 | 18m++8sm+10st |
| *V. cristata* | 38 | 76.50 | 2.01/0.36 | 50.00 | 32.03 | 24m+6sm+8st |
| *V. liouvillei* | 38 | 74.00 | 1.95/0.46 | 33.33 | 38.51 | 26m+8sm+4st |
| *V. pumila* | 40 | 86.50 | 2.16/0.63 | 33.33 | 38.15 | 24m+4sm+6st |
| *V. stangeana* | 38 | 84.50 | 2.22/0.56 | 41.67 | 38.46 | 28m+8sm+2st |
| *V. tessellata* | 38 | 77.00 | 2.03/0.56 | 36.36 | 35.71 | 22m+2sm+14st |
| *V. testacea* | 38 | 88.00 | 2.41/0.56 | 41.67 | 38.64 | 30m+8sm |

st - standard deviation; m - median; sm - submedian; st - subterminal

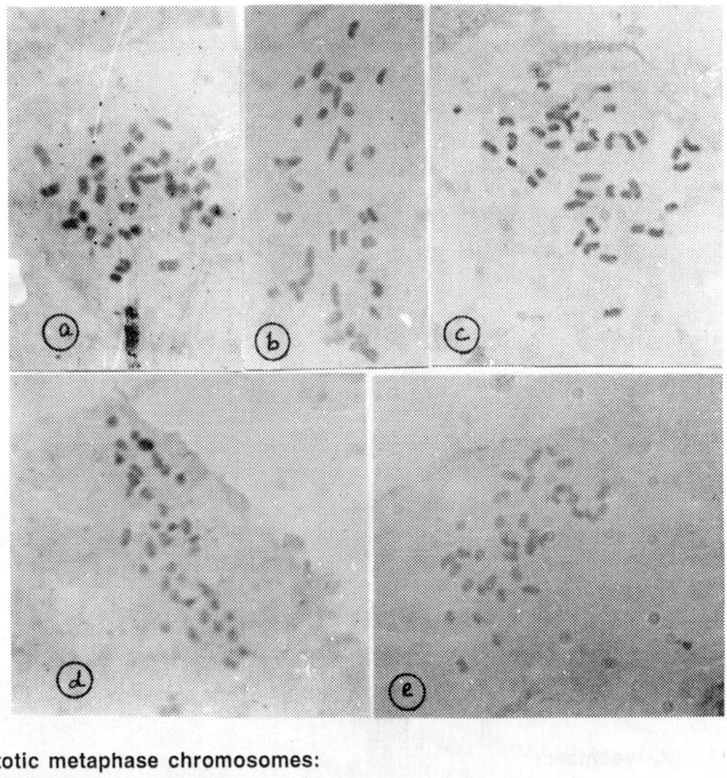


**Plate 7.1: Mitotic metaphase chromosomes:**

(a) *V.alpina* (2n = 38); (b) *V.bicolor* (2n = 38); (c) *V.coerulea* (2n = 38); (d) *V.coerulescens* (2n = 36); (e) *V.cristata* (2n = 38).

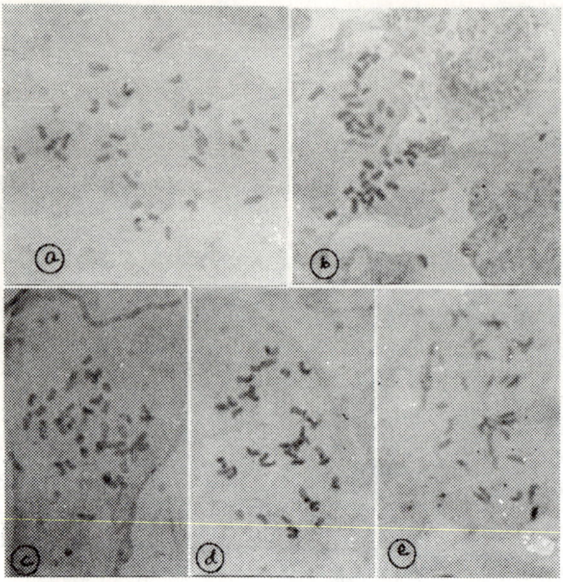


**Plate 7.2: Mitotic metaphase chromosomes:**

(a) *V.liouvillei* (2n = 38); (b) *V.pumila* (2n = 40); (c) *V.stangeana* (2n = 38); (d) *V.tessellata* (2n = 36); (e) *V.testacea* (2n = 38).

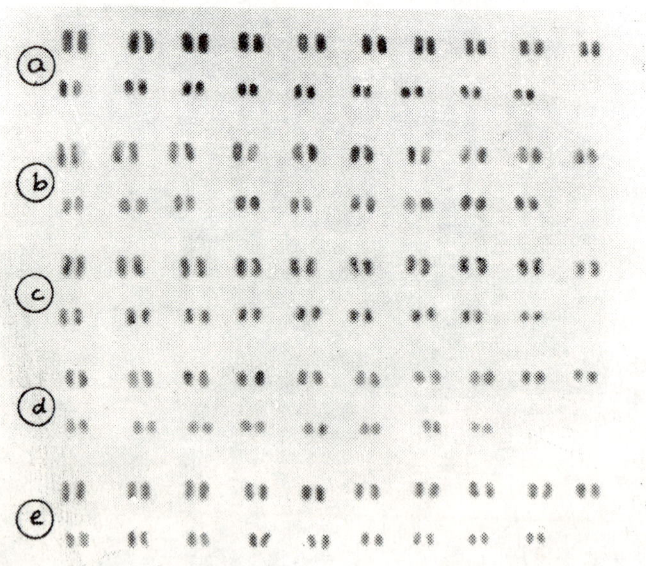


**Plate 7.3: Karyotypes:**

(a) *V.alpina* (2n = 38); (b) *V.bicolor* (2n = 38); (c) *V.coerulea* (2n = 38); (d) *V.coerulescens* (2n = 36); (e) *V.cristata* (2n = 38).

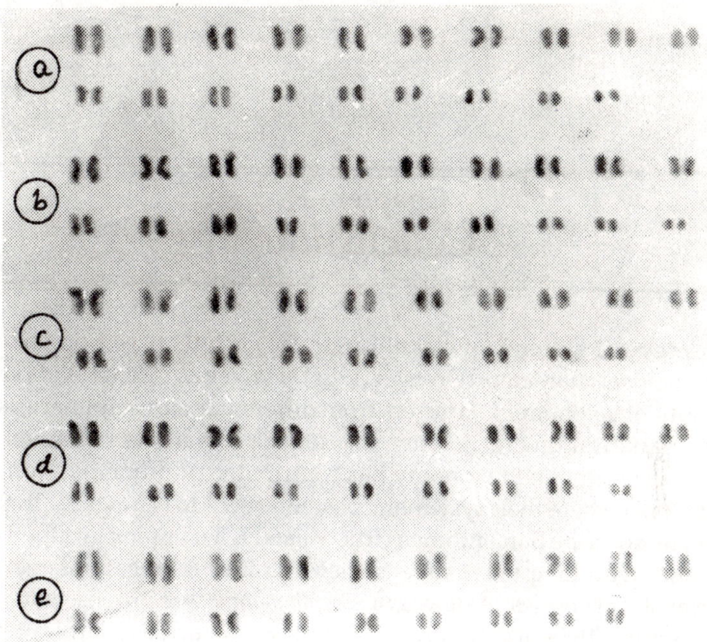


**Plate 7.4: Karyotypes:**

(a) *V.liouvillei* (2n = 38); (b) *V.pumila* (2n = 40); (c) *V.stangeana* (2n = 38); (d) *V.tessellata* (2n = 36); (e) *V.testacea* (2n = 38).

# Chapter - 8
# Conclusion

There are several systems of classification for orchids based on conventional macromorphological characters (Dressler, 1981). However, recent trends emphasise additional input of taxonomic characters from different interdisciplinary aspects for phylogenetic classification and solving taxonomic problems of controversial taxa. Consequenlty, experimental taxonomy has contributed additional information for some complex taxa where their systematic position needs to be revised. In the family orchidaceae, the subtribe Sarcanthinae (true *Vanda*) is a complex group. Therefore, several authors have attempted to suggest their affinities, segregations, merger of the genera and transfer of species. A new genus *Papilionanthe* was proposed by Schlechter (1926) and Holttum (1959) for the terete leaved *Vanda* which was later supported by Garay proposed by Shindo & Kamemoto (1963), and Garay (1974). In 1986, Garay proposed to erect a new genus *Trudelia* to include three species viz., *T. alpina* (Lindl.) Garay, an Indian species (*V.alpina* Lindl.); *T. Griffithii* (Lindl.) Garay; and *T. chlorosantha* Garay. Senghas (1990) further suggested to include *V. cristata* dn *V. pumila* in *Trudelia*. However, *Trudelia* as a distinct genus is being debated and is still considered aberrant South Indian species *V. spathulata* Spreng. As a result, *Vanda* has become a controversial group, and the present investigation has made an attempt to perceive the confusion created by this genus.

Present investigation revealed that out of 40 species which are mainly distributed in the Indo-Malayan region, India is known to possess 12 species namely, *V. alpina, V. bensonii, V. bicolor, V. coerulea, V. coerulescens, V. cristata, V. liouvillei, V. pumila, V. stangeana, V. testacea* and *V. wightii*. *V. wightii* which is endemic to Nilgiri Hills is considered to be extinct as this species has not been rediscovered in nature ever since Wight's collection. During the present investigation, *V. bensonii* could not be located from their reported habitat and hence, may be very rare or is on the verge of extinction. Of the 10 species that were collected, *V. bicolor* is a lesser known species which is restricted to sub-Himalayan range including the Himalayan Kingdom of Bhutan. On the other hand, *V. alpina, V. bensonii, V. cristata, V. coerulescens, V. liouvillei, V. pumila, V. stangeana* are distributed over the Himalayan rnage including the Indo-Chinese and the Indo-Burmese regions. Eight of the collected species viz., *V. alpina, V. bicolor, V. coerulea, V. coerulescens, V. cristata, V. liouvillei, V. pumila, V. stangeana* and the supposedly extinct *V. bensonii* are confined to the northeastern India only, while remaining three species, *V. tessellata, V. testacea* and the so far unsighted *V. wightii* are distributed upto the Western Ghats.

Thus, phytogeographically, distribution of Indian *Vanda*s suggest affinity of Northeastern flora with Indo-Burmese and Indo-Chinese flora. This taxon having a maximum number of species and diversity within the species from the Northeastern region, particularly in the case of *V. alpina, V. coerulea, V. cristata, V. stangeana* and *V. tessellata* suggest Himalayan/Northeastern origin or centre of dispersion.

Phenological observations revealed that there are broadly two flowering seasons among the species of *Vanda*. Majority of the species viz., *V. bicolor, V. coerulescens, V. cristata, V. liouvillei, V. pumila, V. stangeana, V. tessellata* and *V. testacea* flower between spring to early summer (April-June). On the other hand, two species, *V. alpina* and *V. coerulea* flowers from late summer to autumn (July-November). The variation of flowering among the species reveal the optimum requirement for temperature, rainfall, relative humidity, photoperiod and the genetic factors. Longevity of flowers vary from species to species, which is found to be directly related to the nature of their perianth parts (fleshy) and flower size (smaller). Browning on the seed pod takes place from October to January, except for *V. coerulea* which occurs in July-Augusts thereby delaying the retention period. Dehiscence of the seed od occurs from February to April in all the species, which provides a better chance for wind dispersal. All these information are important in systematic studies as well as conservation of the species.

Palynological studies revealed that the shape of the pollinia are ovoid and pollen grains are organised into two distinct pollinia consisting of two unequal lobes. The accessory structures such as viscidium, stipe and caudicle was also paresnet. The pollen grains are packed together compactly within the pollinium as different form of tetrads - decussate, rhomboidal, tetrahedral, linear or massulae which is an indication of an advanced trait. In all the species pollen grains wre aperturate and they were of poroid type which is found in monandrous group of orchids. The surface pattern of pollens varies from psilate for *V. alpina, V. bicolor, V. coerulea, V. coerulescens, V. pumila, V. tessellata* to foveolate for *V. cristata, V. liouvillei, V. stangeana* indicating that *Vanda* species possess advanced character with respect to pollen morphology. This comparative study of pollen organization and morphology can provide data for systematic and phylogenetic utility.

Morphometric studies of the seeds revealed that in all the species the seeds were fusiform shaped and the surface structure have smooth periclinal testa walls, strongly raised anticlinal cell walls. A consistent arrangement of tests cells i.e., long medial cells, short apical chalazal cells suggest orchids-type in the seed classes. Seed length showed more variation compared to seed width suggesting that during maturation the seed elongate due to an increase in testa cell length but not testa cell number. Variation was also more in embryo length but less so in its width, suggesting that variation in embryo volume is due to length rather than width. Hence, during speciation the seed becomes elongated but the diameter did not increase proportionately. The percentage of airspace present could not be correlated to the distribution pattern of the species contrary to the claims by some authors (Arditti *et al.*, 1979; Partick *et al.*, 1980). Therefore, the distribution of the species may be closely related to thier nutritional complexities and complimentary relationship with the surrounding vegetation and climate. This studies can elucidate systematic relationship and also explain certain aspects of orchid seed biology.

Cytological studies revealed that *V. alpina, V. bicolor, V. coereulea, V. cristata, V. liouvillei, V. stangena, V. tessellata* and *V. testacea* possess 2n=38 chromosomes, while *V. coerulescens* and *V. pumila* possess 2n=36 and 2n=40 respectively. In the case of *V. bicolor* and *V. liouvillei*, chromosome number of 2n=38 has been reported for the first time. The difference between the mean chromosome length among the species is 0.6um suggesting thereby that they are closely related species. The chromosomes were mostly median to submedian with few sub-sterminal centromeric chromosomes. Unlike in the evolutionary hierarchy, in orchids highly evolved groups possess median to sub-median chromosomes which was also found in *Vanda* species. Both S% and TF% values has enhanced the karyotype symmetry in the *Vanda* species. Species with the same chromosome number, their karyotype were found to be distinctive, which is a good taxonomic marker. These karyotype details can account for their specific status in the genus *Vanda*. Therefore, the chromosome number and karyotype details is useful in taxonomy as for example, medium to short chromosomes with high basic set are characteristic of advanced features in *Vanda*.

Present work have provided a compreshensive account on Indian species of *Vanda* mainly based on field exploration and studying thelive specimens. Important works on Indian orchids have also been consulted. This work has provided a key to the species for easy identification along with their occurrence, distribution, endemism, extinctiona nd notes on important observation, which is not only important inthe academic filed but also of applied value.

The transfer of *V. spathulata* to *Taprobanea* which was based on pollinarium and vegetative charactes can be justified. But, based on the data derived from different aspects like phenology, palynology, seed morphometry and cytology, showing affinities of characters among the species, it is inferred that the proposal to erect a new genus *Trudelia* for the three species viz., *V. alpina, V. cristata* and *V. pumila* can not be accepted.

**Table - 8.1 : List of Indian species of *Vanda* : present status**

| *Species still retained under* Vanda | | *Species transferred from the genus* Vanda | |
|---|---|---|---|
| *Species* | *Synonyms* | *Species* | *Present status* |
| *V. alpina* | *Trudelia alpina* | *V. spathulata* | *Taprobanea spathulata* (L.) E.A.Christ |
| V. bensonii | | | |
| *V. bicolor* | | *V. hookeriana* | *Paplionanthe hookeriana* (Reichb.f.) Garay |
| *V. coerulea* | | *V. amesiana* | *Holcoglossum amesiana* (Reichb.f.) Christ. |
| *V. coerulescens* | | *V. parishii* | *Hygrochilus parishii* (Veitch & Reichb.f.) Engl. & Prantl. |
| *V. cristata* | *Trudelia cristata* | *V. undulata* | *Vandopsis undulalata* (Lindley) J.J.Sm. |
| *V. liouvillei* | | | |
| *V. pumila* | *Trudelia pumila* | | |
| *V. stangeana* | | | |
| *V. tessellata* | *V. roxburghii* | | |
| *V. testacea* | *V. parviflora* | | |
| V. thwaitesii | Aerida tessellatum | | |
| *V. wightii* | | | |

# Bibliography


Ackerman, J.D. 1986. Mechanisms and evolution of food-deceptive pollination systems in orchids. **Lindleyana**, 1: 108-113.

Ackerman, J.D. 1990. Short- and long-term limitations to fruit production in a tropical orchid. **Ecology**, 71(1): 263-272.

Ackerman, J.D. and Williams, N.H. 1980. Pollen morphology of the tribe Neottiae and its impact on the classification of the Orchidaceae. **Grana**, 19: 7-18.

Ackerman, J.D. and Williams, N.H. 1981. Pollen morphology of the Chloraeinae (Orchidaceae: Diurideae) and Related Subtribes. **Am. J. Bot.**, 68(10): 1392-1402.

Abraham, A. and Vatsala, P. 1981. **An Introduction to Orchids**, RBGRI, Palode, Trivandrum, India.

Aitken, Y. 1974. **Flowering time, climate and genotype : The adaptationn of agricultural species to climate through flowering responses.** Melbourne University Press, Melbourne.

Alberto, F. and Rossi, R. 1988. **Simon & Schulter's Guide to Orchids** (ed. Stanley Schuler). Simon & Schulter Inc. New York. pp. 10-39.

Allison, A.S. and Dennis F.W. 1989. Costs of flowers and fruit production in *Tipularai discolor* (Orchidaceae). **Ecology**, 70(5): 1286-1293.

Arditti, J. 1967. Factors affectging the germination of orchid seed. **Bot. Rev.**, 33: 1-97.

Arditti, J. 1979. Aspects of Orchid physiology. In: **H. Wollhouse (ed.), Advances in botancial research**, Vol. 7. Academic Press, London.

Arditti, J. and Michaud, J.D. 1979. Native orchid seeds. **Golden Gardens**, 48: 8-9,.

Arditti, J., Michaud, J.D., and Healey, P.L. 1979. Morphometry of orchid seeds. I. *Paphiopedilum* and native California and related species of *Cypripedium*. **Am. J. Bot.**, 66(10): 1128-37.

Arditti, J., Michaud, J.D., and Healey, P.L., 1980. Morphometry of orchid seeds. II. Native California and related species of *Calypso, Cephalenthera, Corallorhiza* and *Epipactis*. **Am. J. Bot.**, 67: 347-361.

Arends, J.C. 1970. Cytological observations on genome homology in eight interspecific hybrids of *Phalaenopsis*. **Genetica**, 41:88-100.

Arora, C.M. 1971. In IOPB chromosome number reports. **Taxon**, 19: 102-113.

Arora, Y.K. and Mukherji, A. 1983. **Ornamental orchids of North-East India**. ICAR, Shillong.

Arora, S. 1985. Pollinia of two tropical orchids - A scanning electron microscopre study. **Phytomorph**, 35 (3&4): 161-166.

Arora, S. 1986. Anther and pollen of some Indian Orchids. Scanning and Light Microscope Investigation. Ph.D. Thesis. University of Delhi, Delhi, India.

Arora, S. and Kapil, R.N. 1989. Comparative study of pollinia of two species of *Pholidota* Lindl. **Phytomorph**, 39.

Arora, S. and Kapil, R.N. 1990. Some fascinating features of orchid pollen. **J. Orchid Soc. India**, 4(1,2): 09-28.

Balogh, P. 1979. Pollen morphology of the tribe Cranichideae Endlicher subtribe Spiranthinane Bentham (Orchidaceae), **Orquidea**, 7: 241-260.

Balogh, P. 1982. Genetric redefinition in subtribe Spiranthinae (Orchidaceae); **Am. J. Bot.**, 69: 1119-1132.

Balogh, P. 1982b. Morfologia de polinario ge orchidaceae Maxicanas I Sub-tribe Laelinae. **Orguidea**, 8: 327-42.

Barthlott, W. 1976. Morphologie der samen von Orchideen in Hinblick auf taxonomische aud functionelle aspecte. **Proc. 8th World Orchid Conf.**, Frankfurt, 1975. pp. 444-455.

Barthlott, W. 1981. Epidermanl and seed surface characters of plants systematic applicability and some evolutionary aspects **Nord. J. Bot.**, 1: 345-355.

Barthlott, W. 1984. Microstructural features of seed surfaces. **In Current Concepts in Plant Taxonomy**, Heywood, V.H. and Moore, D.M. (eds), 95-105. Academic Press, London.

Barthlott, W. and Ziegler, B. 1981. Mikromorphologie der Samenschalen als systematische Merkmal bei Orchideen. Berichte Deutsche Botanische Gesellschaft, 94: 267-273.

Battaglia, E. 1957a. A new "5 minutes-fixation" in chromosome analysis. **Caryologia**, 9: 368-370.

Battaglia, E. 1957b. A simplified Feulgen method using cold hydrolysis. **Caryologia**, 9: 372-373.

Deer, J.G. 1863. Beitrage zur Morphologie and Biologie der Familie der Orchideen. Druck and Verlag Von Carl Gerold's Sohn. Vienna.

Benson, L.D. 1962. **Plant Taxonomy: Methods and Principles**. Ronald Press, New York.

Berry, P.E. and Calvo, R.N. 1991. Polinator limitation and position dependent fruit set in th high Andean corchid *Myrosmodes cohleasre* (orchidaceae). **Plant Systematics and Evolution**, 174: 93-101.

Benzing, D.H. and Atwood Jr., J.T. 1984. Orchidaceae: ancestral habitats and current status in forest canopies. **Syst. Bot.**, 9: 155-165.

Bhat, D.M. 1992. Phenology of tree species of tropical moist forest of Uttara Kannada district, Karanataka, India, **J. Biosci.**, 17(3): 325-352.

Biswas, B.K. 1986. Cytological studies in few cultivars of Indian Lady's slippers (*Paphiopedilum* Pftiz.) In: **Biology, Conservation and Culture of Orchids** (ed. S.P. Vij), Affiliated East West Press, New Delhi.

Bose, T.K. and Yadav, L.P. 1986. Physiology of flowering in orchids. **Biology, Conservation and Culture of Orchids** (Ed.S.P.Vij), pp. 79-83. Affiliated East West Press, New Delhi.

Brieger, F.G. 1975. On the Orchid system; General Principles and the disctinction of sub families. **Proc. 8th World Orchid Conf.**, Frankfurt.

Brown, R. 1810. Prodromus flora Nova Hollandia et insula Van-Die-men. J. Johnson, London.

Brown, R. 1820. *Vanda* roxburghii. **Bot. Reg.**, 6: t.506.

Brown, R. 1821-22. Bot. Reg. t.573.

Burgeff, H. 1936. Samenkeinung ger orchideen und Entwichlung ihrer Keimpflangeen. **Gustav Fischer Verlag,** Jena.

Burns-Balogh, P. 1983. A theory on the evolution of the exinie in Orchidaceae; **Am. J. Bot.,** 70: 1304-1312.

Burns-Balogh, P. and Funk, V.A. 1986. A phylogenetic analysis of the Orchidaceae. Şmithsonian Contributions to Botany, 61:1-79.

Burns-Balogh, P. and Hesse, M. 1988. Pollen morphology of the Cypripedioid orchids. **Pl. Syst. Evol.**, 158: 165-182.

Caprio, J.M. 1973. The solar thermal unit concept in problems related to plant development and potential evapotranspiration. In: H. Leight (ed.), Phenology and Seasonality Modelling. Sring-er-Verlag, New York. pp. 353-364.

Chadha, K.L. 1992. The Indian orchid scenario. **J. Orchid Soc. India,** 6(1,2): 1-4.

Changkija, S., Kumar, Y. and Gurung, P.B. 1992. **Orchids of Nagaland.** Forest Department, Nagaland.

Chardard, R. 1963. Contribution a btude cytotaxonomisque des orchidees. **Rev. Cytol. et Biol. Veg.**, 25: 1-58.

Chardard, R. 1971. Fine structure of tapetal cells, microsporocytes and pollen grains in some orchids; **Am. Univ. A.R.E.R.S.**, 9: 154-178.

Chase, M.W.K., Camiron, M. Hills, H.G. and Jarrell, J. (In press). DNA sequence and phylogenetic of the Orchidaceae and other liliod monocots. In Proceeding of the 14th World Orchid Conference, Glascow, 1993. Her Majesty's Stationery Office. Glascow.

Chase, M.W.K. and Pippen, J.S. 1988. Seed morphology in the Oncidiinae and related subtribes (Orchidacease). **Syst. Bot.**, 13: 313-323.

Chase, M.W.K. and Pippen, J.S. 1990. Seed morphology and phylogeny in subtribe Catasetinae (Orchidaceae), **Lindleyana,** 5: 126-134.

Chatterjee, D. 1940. Studies on the endemic flora of India and Burma, **J. Asiat. Soc. Bengal,** 5(1): 19-67.

Chatterji, A.K. 1986. Chromosomes in orchid phylogeny and classificationj. **Biology, Conservation and Culture of Orchids** (S.P. Vij, ed), pp. 181-187.

Chatterji, A.K. 1990. Chromosomal relationships and evolution of some sarcanthine ochids. **J. Orchid Soc. India,** 4(1,2): 135-143.

Chauhan, A.S. 1984. *Vanda jainii* Chauhan - A new orchid species from Meghalaya, **J. Econ., Tax. Bot.**, 5(4): 977-979.

Cheng. S. and Tang. Z. 1986. A revision of the genus *Vanda* (Orchidaceae) of China. **Acta Bot. Yunnan,** 8(2): 216+221 (repr. in transl., Orchid Digest. 52: 38-46. 1988).

Christenson, E.A. 1992. Notes on Asiatic orchids. **Lindleyana,** 7:88-94.

Clifford, H.T. and Smith, W.K. 1969. Seed morphology and classification of Orchidaceae. **Phytomorph,** 19: 133-139.

Close, R.C., Moar, N.T., Tomlinson, A.I., and Lowe, A.D. 1978. Aerial dispersal of biological material from Australia to New Zealand. **Int. J. Biometer,** 22: 1-19.

Cole, F.R. and Firmage, D.H. 1984. The Floral Ecology of *Platanthera blephariglottis*. **Am. J. Bot.,** 71: 700-710.

Constance, L. and Chuang. T.I. 1982. SEM survey of pollen morphology and classification in Hydrophyllaceae (Water family). **Am. J. Bot.**, 69: 40-53.

Davis, P.H. and Heywood, V.H. 1963. **Principles of Plant Taxonomy**. Oliver and Boyd, Edinburgh and London.

Deb, D.B. 1983. The flora of Tripura state. Vol. 2. **Orchideceae**. Today and Tomorrow's printers and Publishers, New Delhi. pp. 446-67.

Dressler, R.L. 1981. **The Orchids, Natural History and Classification**. Harvard Univ. Press, Cambridge.

Dressler, R.L. 1986. Recent advances in orchid phylogeny. **Lindleyana**, 1: 5-20.

Dressler, R.L. 1990a. Recent advances in orchid phylogeny. **Lindleyana**, 5: 102-109.

Dressler, R.L. 1990b. The Spiranthoideae a grade or subfamily? **Lindleyana**, 5: 110-116.

Drssler, R.L. 1990C. The major clades of the Orchidaceae - Epidenroideae. **Lindleyana**, 5: 117-125.

Deressler, R.L. 1993. **Phylogeny and classification of the orchid family**. Dioscorides Press, Portland.

Drugg. W.S. 1962. Pollen morphology of the Lennoaceae. **Am. J. Bot.**, 49: 1027-1032.

Duncan, R.E. 1959. Orchids and Cytology. In: **The Orchids: A Scienfitic Survey** (ed. C.L. Withner), Ronald Press, New York.

Elisens, W.J. 1985. The systematic significance of seed coat anatomy among New World species of tribe Antirrhineae (Scorphulariaceae) **Syst. Bot.**, 10: 282-299.

Elisens, W.J. and A. S. Tomb. 1983. Seed morpholgy in new World Antirrhineae (Scrophulariaceae): Systematic and phylogenetic implications. **Plant syst. Evol.**, 142: 23-47.

Erdtman, G. 1952. **Pollen Morphology and plant Taxonomy**. Stockholm.

Freudnstein, V.J. and Rasmussem, N.F. 1996. Pollinium Development and Number in the Orchidaceae, **Am. J. Bot.**, 813-824.

Garay, L.A. 1960. On the origin of the orchidaceae. I. **Bot. Mus. Leaflets**, harvard, 19: 57-96.

Garay, L.A. 1986. *Trudelia* a new name for V. alpina. **Orchid Dig.**, 50(2): 73-77.

Ghatak, J. and Devi, R.K.J. 1986. Orchids of Manipur. In: **Biology, conservation and culture of orchids**. (ed. S.P. Vij). East-West Press, New Delhi. pp. 357-62.

Gilbert, E.F. 1961. Phenology of sumacs. **Am. Midland Natur.**, 66: 286-300.

Grant, B. 1895. **The Orchids of Burma**. The Hanthawaddy Press, Rangoon.

Harley, M.M. 1968a. The nature of the endoaperture in the pollen of the Sapotaceae. pp. 417-419. In: S. Blackmore and I.K. Ferguson (eds.). **Pollen and Spores: Form and function**. Academic press, London.

Harley, M.M. 1968b. Distinguishing pollen characters forthe Sapotaceae. **Canad. J. Bot.**, 64: 3091-3100.

Haridasan, K. and Rao, R.R. 1985. Forest Flora and Meghalaya. 1. I-VIII: 10451. Dehradun.

Harper, J.N., Lovell, P.H. and Moore, K.G. 1970. The shapes and sizes of seed. **Ann. Rev. Syst. Ecol.**, 1:327-356.

Haas, H.F. 1877. Asymbiontische Vermehrung euro-paischer Erdorchidden. 1. *Dactylorrhiza* sambucina (L) Soo. Dieorchidee 28:27-31.

Healey, P.L., Michaud, J.D. and Arditti, J. 1980. Morphometry of orchid seeds. III. Native California and related species of *Goodyera, Piperia, Platanthera* and *Spiranthes*. **Am. J. Bot.**, 67: 508-518.

Heather, C.P. and Lawrence, D.H. 1995. Effect of pollination success on floral longevity in the orchid *Calypso bulbosa* (orchidaceae) **Am. J. Bot.**, 82(9): 1131-1136.

Hegde, S.N. 1980. Preliminary observations and list of Orchids of Arunachal Pradesh. **Arunachal For. News**, 3(3): 1-11.

Hegde, S.N. 1984. **Orchids of Arunachal Pradesh**. Forest Deptt. Arunahcal Pradesh, Itanagar.

Hegde, S.N. 1985. Observations on the habitat distribution of orchids of Arunachal Pradesh, **Journ. Bombay. Natr. Hist**. Soc., 82(1): 114-125.

Hegde, S.N. 1987a. Development of Orchidology as plant and cut flower trade industry in the North-Eastern vis-a-vis Arunachal Pradesh. **Arunachal For. News**, 5: 52-66.

Hegde, S.N. 1987b. Progress in Orchid Research and Development in Arunachal Pradesh: A Report, **Arunachal For. News**, 6: 11-18.

Hegde, S.N. and Ingalhalli, R.N. 1985. In: 10PB chromosome number reports. **Taxon**, 34: 546-57.

Hesse, M. 1986. An exine architecture model for viscin threads. **Granna**, 23: 69-75.

Hesse, M. and Burns-Balogh, P. 1984. Pollen and Pollianrium morphology of *Habenaria* (Orchidaceae). **Pollen Spores**, 26: 285-400.

Heywood, V.H. 1996. Biodiversity conservation: an eco-biogeographical approach. In: **Indo-British Workshop on Biodiversity, Conservation and Evaluation**. TBGRI, Trivandrum, India, pp. 46-58.

Hideki, T.1993. Seed morphology and its systematic implications in Pyroloideae (Ericeceae), **Int. J. Pl. Sci**., 154(1): 175-186.

Holtum, R.E. 1959. Evolutionary trends in the Scarthinae orchids. **Am. Orchid Soc. Bull**., 28: 747-54.

Hooker, J.D. 1895. A centruy of Indian Orchids. **Ann. Roy. Bot. Gard**., Cal. 5: Bengal Secretariat Press, Calcutta.

Hufford, L. 1988. Seed morphology of *Eucnide* and other Lossaceae. **Syst. Bot.**, 13: 154-167.

Jackson, M.T. 1966. Effects of microclimate on spring flowering phenology. **Ecology**, 43(3): 407-415.

Jain, S.K. and Sastry, A.R.K. 1980. **Threatened plants of India - a state of art report**. Howrah.

Jain, S.K. and Hajra, P.K. 1976. Orchids in some protected habitats in Assam, Easter India, **Am. Orchid Soc. Bull**., 45: 1103-09.

Jain, S.K. and Mehrotra, A. 1984. **A preliminary inventory of Orchidaceae in India**, BSI, Howrah.

Janzen, D.H. 1967. Synchronization of sexula reproductioin of trees within the dry season in Central Amercia. **Evolution**, 21: 620-637.

Janzen, D.H. 1977. A note on optimal mate selection by plant. **Am. Nat**. 111: 305-371.

Javier, A.R., Eliva, J.M. and Ackerman, J.D. 1992. Effects of disply size, flowering phenology and nectar availability on effective visitation frequency in *Comparettia fulcata* (Orchidaceae). **Am. J. Bot.**, 79(9): 1009-1017.

Jones, W. 1795. *Vanda* **Asiat. Res.** IV.302.

Joy, K.A. 1992. Studies on *Paphiopedilum* Pfitz. of Nothereastern Region of India. M.Phil. dissertation, North Eastern Hill University, Shillong.

Joy, K.A., Sharma, J. and Kumar Y. 1994. Reproductive biology of Lady's Slipper *Paphiopedilum* - A potential orchid groups for floriculture in India. In : **Floriculture Techniques, Trade and Trends**. IBH and Oxford Publ., New Delhi.

Joy, K.A. 1996. Experimental Taxonomy of *Paphiopedilum* Pfitz. of North eastern region of India. Ph.D. dissertation, NEHU, Shillong.

Kamemoto, H. 1961. Chromosome numbers of orchids in Hawaii. **Hawaii, Agri. Expt. Station Bull.**, 27: 5-28.

Kamemotor, H., Tanaka, R. and Kosaki, K. 1961. Chromosome numbers of orchids in Hawaii. **Hawaii Agri. Exp. Station Bull.**, 127: 5-28.

Kamemotor, H. and R. sagarik. 1975. **Beautiful Thai Orchid Species**, Bangkok. pp. 171.

Kapil, R.N. and S. Arora, 1990. Some fascinating features of orchid pollen. **J. Orchid Soc. Ind.**, 4(1,2): 09-28.

Karasawa, K. and Saito, K. 1982. A revision of the genus *Paphiopedilum* **Bull. Hiroshima Bot. Gard.**, 5: 1-69.

Karthikeyna, S.K., Jain, S.K. Nayar, M.P. and Sanjappa. 1989. **Flora Indica Enumeratio: Monocotyledonae**, BSI, Howrah.

Kataki, S.K. Jain, S.K. and Sastry, A.R.K. 1984. Distribution of orchids of Sikkim and North-Eastern India. **Plant Conserv. Bull.**, 5: 1-38.

Kataki, S.K. 1986. **Orchids Flora of Meghalaya**. Forest Department, Shillong.

Kaul, V. and Rainai, R. 1980. The Phenlology of woody agniosperms in Srinagar. **Ind. For.**, 106(2): 94-101.

Kennedy, G.C. 1979. Some Monopodial Orchids. The Genera: *Vanda, Euanthe, Paplionanthe, Hygrochilus, Vandopsis, Esmeralda, Aridis, Arachmis, Seidenfadia, Rhynchilus, Anota, Ascocentrum* and *Renonthera*. Orch. Did., pp.45-50.

Khoshoo, T.N. 1995. Census of Indias Biodiversity : Tasks ahead. **Curr. Sci.** 69(1): 14-17.

Khoshoo, T.N. 1996. Biodiverstiy conservation and sustainable utilization: A blutprint for Action. In: **Indo-British Workshop on Biodiversity, Conservation and Evaluation**. TBGRI, Trivandrum, India. pp. 12-29.

Kim, E.S., Whitehead, V.B. and Johnson, S.D. 1994. Floral and pollinator divergence in two sexually deceptive south African orchids. **Am. J. Bot.**, 81(2): 185-194.

King, G. and Pantling, R. 1898. The orchids of the Sikkim Himalaya. **Ann. Roy. Bot. Gard.**, Calcutta, 8: 1-342.

Krach, J.E. 1977. Seed characters and affinites among the Saxifragineae. **Plant Syst. Evol.**, (Suppl.): 141-153.

Krishnaswamy, V.S. and Mathuda, G.S. 1954. Pehnological behaviour of a few forest species at New Forest, Dehra Dun, **Ind. For.**, 80: 124-53; 187-206.

Kumar, Y., Limasenla and Sharma, J. 1997. Indians *Vanda*s - II: Biodiversity and Sustainable Use. **J. Orchid. Sco. India**, 11(1-2); 85-91.

Kumar, Y. and J. Sharma, 1992. The orchids of North-East India: Towards 'A Rainbow Revolution'. **J. Orchid Soc. India**, 6(1,2): 21-25.

Kumar, Y. Sharma, J. and George, M.. 1994. Biodiversity of North east India: A Promising challenge to biotechnologists. In: **Biotechnology: its prospects in North East** (ed. S. Sharma), pp. 80-86. Gauhati Universtiy, Gauhati.

Larry, H. 1995. Seed morphology of Hydrangeaceae and its phylogenetic implications. **Int. J. Plant Sci.**, 156(4): 555-580.

Lawrence, G.H.M. 1955. **An Introduction to Plant Taxonomy**, Central Book Depot, Allahabad.

Leith, H. 1970. Pehnology in productivity studies. In: **Analyasis of Temperate Forest Ecosystems**, D. Reichle, ed. Heidelberg. Spriner-Verlag.

Leith, H. 1974. Purpose of a phenology book. In: Phenology book. In: **Phenology and Seasonality modelling** (Ed. Berlin Springer-Verlag), pp. 3-19.

Leith, H. and Radford, J.S. 1971. Phenology, resource management and synagraphis computer mapping. **Bio. Sci**. 21: 62-70.

Levan, A., Fredga, K. and Sanberg. A.A. 1964. Nomenclature for centromeric position on chromosomes. **Heriditas**. 52: 201-200.

Lewis, H. 1957. Genetics and cytology in relation to Taxonomy. **Taxon**, 6: 42-46.

Lindley, J. 1826. Orchidearum sceletos. Richard Taylor, London.

Linnaeus, K. Von. 1753. **Species Plantarum**.

Loomis, R.S. and Coonor, D.J. 1992. **Crop ecology: Productivity and management in agriculature systems**. Cambridge Univ. Press, New York.

Maheshwari, P. 1950. **An Introduction to the Embryology of the Angiosperms**, Mc Graw-Hill, New York.

Maheshwari, J.K. 1995. **Orchids of India**. Scientific Publishers, Jodpur.

Manilal, K.S. and Kumar, C.S. 1986. Researches on Indian orchids a review. In: **Biology, Conservation and Culture or orchids** (ed. S.P. Vij). Affiliated East-West Press, New Delhi.

Manilal, K.S. and Kumar, C.S. 1994. **A catalogue of Indian Orchids**. Bishen Singh and Mahendra Pal Singh, Dehradun.

Martin, R.M. 1988. Unraveling a Rainbow 1. A brief histroy of *Vanda* hybridizing. **Am. Orch. Soc. Bull.**, 57(7). 709-718.

Matthews, J. and Levins, P.A. 1986. The systematic significance of seed morphology in *Ortulaca* (Portulacaceae) under scanning electron microscopy. **Syst. Bot.**, 11: 302-308.

McMillan, C. 1957. Nature of the plant community. IV. Phenological variation within five woodland communities under controlled temperatures. **Am. J. Bot.**, 44: 157-163.

McMillan, C. and Pagel, B.F. 1958. Phenological variationi within a population of *Symphoricarpos occidentalis*. **Ecology**, 39: 766-770.

Mehra, P.N. and Sehgal, R.N. 1980. In: IOPB Chromosome number reports. **Taxon**, 29: 347-67.

Mehra, P.N. and Kashyap, S.K. 1976. In: IOPB Chromosome numbe reports. **Taxon**, 25: 483-500

Mehra, P.N. and Kashyap, S.K. 1984d. Cytological observations on some west Himalayan orchids Tribe: Epidendreae. III. Subtribes: Cyrtopodiinae, Sarcanthinae. **Cytologia**, 49: 613-27.

Mehra, P.N. and Vij, S.P. 1970. In: IOPB Chromosome number reports. **Taxon**, 19: 102-113.

Melampy, M.N. 1987. Flowering phenology. pollen flow and fruit production in the Andean shrub, *Befaria resinosa*. **Occologia**, 73: 293-300.

Modgil, M. 1996. On the pollen morphology of *Rubus ellipticus* SM. A Basic Approach. **Ind. J. For.**, 19(4): 365-367.

Molvray, M. and Kores, J.P. 1995. Charactor analysis of the seed coat in Spirinthoideae and Orchidiodeae, with special reference to the Diurideae (Orchidaceae). **Am. J. Bot.**, 82(11): 1443-1454.

Moore, P.D. Webb, J.A. and Collinson M.E. 1991. **Pollen Analysis**. Blackwell Scienfitic Publications, Oxford.

Mukherjee, S.K. 1983. **Orchids**. ICAR, New Delhi.

Naik, V.N. 1984. **Taxonomy of Angiosperms**. Tata McGraw-Hill Publishig Company Limited, New Delhi.

Nair, P.K.K. 1965. **Pollen grains of W. Himalayan plants**. Asia Publishing House.

Nair, P.K.K. 1974. Glimpses in Plant Research Vol. II - Studies in plant biology - A Palynological Approach.

Nair, P.K.K. 1985. **Essentials of palynology**. M/s Totay and Tommorow's Producers & Publishers, New Delhi.

Nair, P.K.K. 1991. Pollen morphology, Plant Taxonomy and Evolution, **Rheedia**, 1(1,2): 78-83.

Naya, M.P. and Sastry, A.R.K. 1988-1990. Red Data Book of Indian Plants (eds.), Vol. I,II,III, B.S.I., Calcutta.

Ness, B.D. 1989. Seed morphology and taxonomic relationships in *Calochotus* (Liliaceae). **Syst. Bot.**, 14: 495-505.

Newton, G.D. and Williams, H. 1978. Pollen Morphology of Cypripedioideae and Apostasioideae (Orchidaceae). **Selbyana**, 2: 169-182.

Nilsson, L.A. 1978. Pollination ecology and adapatation in *Platanthera chlorantha* (Orchidaceae), **Bot. Not.**, 131: 35-51.

Nilsson, L.A. 1983. Anthecology of *Orchis mascula* (Orchidaceae). **Nordic J. Bot.**, 3: 633-638.

Nilsson, L.A. 1984. Anthecology of *Orchis morio* (Orchidaceae) at its outpost in the north. **Nova Acta. Regiae Societatis Scientiarum Upsaliensis**, 3: 167-179.

Nowicke, J.W. and Miller, J.S. 1989. Pollen morphology and the relationships of Hoplestigmataceae. **Taxon**, 38(1): 12-16.

Opler, P.A., Frankie, C.W. and Baker, H.G. 1980. Comparative phenological study of tree layer and shrub species in tropical west and dry forests in the low lands of Costa Rich. **J. Ecol.**, 68: 167-188.

Patel, V.S., Skvarla, J.J. and Raven, P.H. 1985. Pollen charactes in relation to the delimitation of the Myratles. **Ann. Missouri Bot. Gard.**, 71: 858-956.

Patrick. L.H., Justine, D.M. and Arditti, J. 1980. Morphometry of orchid seeds. III. Native California and related species of *Goodyera, Piperia, Platenthera* and *Spiranthes*. **Am. J. Bot.**, 67(4): 508-518.

Perring, C. 1996. The Value of Biodiversity for Sustainable Economic Development. In: **Indo-British Workshop on Biodiversity, Conservation and Evaluation**. TBGRI, Trivandrum, India, pp. 30-45.

Peter E. Endress. 1994. Floral diversity of selected group - orchidals. In: **Diversity and Evolutionary Biology of Tropical Flowers**. Camridge Univ. Press.

Phukan, S. 1996. *Vanda lioouvillei* Finet. A new record from India. **Orch. Rev.**, 104: 189-190.

Pradhan, U.C. 1979. **Indian Orchids: Guide to Identification and Culcture**. Vol. II, Faridabad.

Primack, R.B., Miao, L. and Becker, K.R. 1994. Costs of reproduction in the Pink Lady's slipper orchid (*Cypripedium acule*) Defoliation, increased fruit production and fire. **Am. J. Bot.**, 81(9): 1083-1090.

Radford, A.E., Dickenson, W.C., Massey, J.R. and C.R. Bill. 1974. **Vascular Plant Systematics**. Harper & Row, New York and London.

Radlkofer, L. 1884. Ueber den systematischen werth der Pollen beschaffenheit bei den Acanthaceen. S.B. Math-phys. Sl., bayer. Akad. Wiss., 13:2(1882) 256-314.

Ralhan, P.K., Khanna, R.K., Singh, S.P. and Singh, J.S. 1985. Phenological characteristics of tree layer of Kumaun Himalayan forests. **Vegetatio**, 60: 91-101.

Rao, R.R. 1986. Florestic Diversity of Eastern Himalaya - A national heritage for conservation. **Proc. Ind. Acad. Sci**. (Suppli.), pp. 133-151.

Rao, R.R. 1998. Biodiversity of North East India - A National Heritage for Conservation. Workshop on Agricultured, Biodiversity and Climate change, N.E.H.U., Abs. Shillong, pp. 7-10.

Rassmussen, F.N. 1982. The gynostemium of the neottioid orchids. **Opera Botanica**, 65: 1-96.

Rassmussen, F.N. 1985. Orchids. IN R.M.T. Dahlgren. H.T. Clifford and P.F. Yeo (eds.), The families of monocotyledons, pp. 249-274. Spring-er-Verlag, Berlin.

Rassmussen, F.N. 1986. Ontogeny and phylogeny in Orchidaceae. **Lindleyana**, 1: 114-124.

Rathcke, B. and Lacey, E.P. 1985. Phenological pattern of terrestial plants. **Annu. Rev. Ecol. Syst.**, 16. 179-214.

Ravi, K. and Pushpangadan, P. 1996. Application of Environmental Valuation Techniques for Economic Evaluation of Biodiversity: A Critical Investigation. In: **Indo-British Workshop on Biodiversity, Conservation and Evaluation**. TBGRI, Trivandrum, India. pp. 134-149.

Ravindran, P.N. 1979. Nuclear behaviour in the strile pollen of *Vanilla planifolia* (Andrews). **Caryologia**, 44: 391-396.

Rawal, R.S., Bankoti, N.S., Samant, S.S. and Pangtey, Y.P.S. 1991. Phenology of tree layer species from the timber line around Kumaun in Central Himalayan, India. **Vegetatio**. 93: 109-118.

Reichenbach, H.G. 1852. De pollinis orchidearum genesi ac structura et de orchideis in artem ac systema reeigendis. Ph.D. dissertation. F. Hofmeister, Leipzig.

Reid, W.V. and Miller, K. 1989. **Keeping option alive. The Scienfic basis for conserving biodiversity**. World Resources Institute. Washington.

Roxbursh, W (Edw. Garay 1832). **Flora Indica** OR desrciption of Indian Plants 3 vol. Sarampore.

Roy, S.C. and Sharma, A.K. 1972. Cytological studies of Indian orchids. **Proc. Ind. Natl. Sci. Acad.**, 38: 72-86.

Sabat M.A. and Ackerman, J.D. 1996. Fruit set in a deceptive orchid. The effect of flowering phenology, display size and floral abundance. **Am. J. Bot.**, 83(9): 1181-1186.

Sampathkumaran, M. and Seshagirian, K.N. 1931. Cytology of the Embryosac in Orchids. **Abst. Proc. 18th Ind. Sci. Cong.**, Nagpur.

Sastry, A.R.K., Kataki, S.K. and Chauhan, A.S. 1983. Threatened plants of North-eastern India. In: **Materials for a catalogue of Threatened Plants of India**, pp. 61-69. Howrah.

Sau, H. and Sharma, A.K. 1983. Chromosome evolution and affinity of certain genera of orchideceae. Cytologia, 48. 363-72.

Schill, R. and W. Pfeiffer. 1977. Untersuchungen an Orchideenopollinien unter besonderer Berucksichtigung inhrer Feinskulpturen. **Pollen et Spores,** 19: 5-118.

Schelchter, R. 1926. Das system der Orchidaceen. Notizblatt. Bot. Garten. Berlin Dahlem. 10: 563.

Schulter, R.E. and Pease, A.S. 1963. **Generic names of Orchids: their origin and meaning.** Academic Press, NewYork, pp. 331.

Seidanfaden, G. 1982. Contribution to the orchid flora of Thailand. **X. Nord. J. Bot**., 2: 193-218.

Seidanfaden, G. 1988. Orchid genera in Thailand 14. Fifty-nine vandoid genera. **Op. Bot**., 95: 5-398.

Seidnafaden, G. 1992. The orchids of Indo China. **Op. Bot.,** 114: 5-502.

Semalty, R.K. and Sharma, C.M. 1996. Phenology and Floral Biology of *Acer caesium* Wall. **Ind. For**., 170-176.

Senghas, K. 1990. Aeridinae. In: R. Schlecter, **Die Orchideen** ed. 3,5 : 1131-1422.

Senghas, K., Ehler, N., Schill, R. and Barthlott, W. 1974. Neue Undersuchungun und Mehoden Zur Systematic und Morphologie der Orchideen. **Die Orchidee** 25: 157-168.

Sharma, A.K. and Chatterji, A.K. 1960. Cytotaxonomy of a few orchid genera. **Proc. Ind. Soc. Cong. 47th session (Bot. Section)**.

Sharma, A.K. and Chatterji, A.K. 1966. Cytological studies on orchids with respect to their volution and affinities. **Nucleus**. 9(2): 177-203.

Sharma, J. 1993. Studieson orchids of North East India: In *Vitro* multiplication and preservation of horticulturally important *Dendrobium* and *Paphiopedilumi species*. Ph.D. these, North-Eastern Hill University, Shillong.

Sharma, J. and Kumar, Y. 1993. Orchids of North-Eastern India. Empashis on orchid industry for trade. **Indian J. Hill Farming**, 6(2): 213-215.

Shekhar, N. 1984. Cytotaxonomic studies in some Indian Orchids (Ph.D. Thesis). Punjab University, Chandigarh.

Shindo, K. and Kamemoto, H. 1963a. Karyotype analysis of some Sarcanthine Orchids. **Am. J. Bot.**, 50: 73-79.

Shindo, K. and Kamemoto, H. 1963b. Chromosome relationships of *Arides* and allied genera. **Am. Orchid Soc. Bull**., 32. 922-26.

Simpson, B.B. 1977. Breeding systems of dominant perennial plants of two disjunct warm desert ecosystems. **Oecologia**, 27:203-226.

Sneath, P.H.A. and Sokal, R.R. 1973. **Numerical Taxonomy**. W.H. Freeman, San Francisco.

Solbrig, O.T. and Yang, T.W. 1977. Strategies in relation to timing of blooming and fruiting. In: G.H. Orians and O.T. Solbrig (eds.), convergent evolution in warm deserts. Dowden, Hutchinson and Ross, Stroudsburg, P.A. pp. 83-99.

Stace, C.A. 1989. **Plant Taxonomy and Biosystematics**, 2nd Ed. Edward Arnold, London.

Stern, K. and Roche, L. 1974. **Genetics of Forest Ecosystem**. Chapman and Hall Ltd. London. pp. 330.

Story, W.B. 1952. Chromosome numbers of some *Vanda* species and Hybrids. Am. **Orchid Soc. Bull.**, 21: 801-806.

Story, W.B., Kamemotor, H. and Shindo, K. 1963. Chromosome of *Vanda spathulata*. **Am. Orchid Soc. Bull.**

Takahashi, H. 1993. Seed morphology and its systematic implications in Pyroloideae (Ericaceae). **Int. J. Plant Sci**. 154: 175-186.

Tanaka, R. and kamemotor, H. 1961. Mjeiotic chromosome behaviour in some inter generic hybrids of the *Vanda* alliances. **Am. J. Bot.**, 48(7): 573-82.

Tara, M. and Kamemotor, H. 1970. Karyotype relationship in Sarcanthinae. **Am. J. Bot.**, 57: 176-182.

Thieret, J. W. 1955. The seeds of *Veronica* and allied genera. **Lloydia**, 18: 37-45.

Thompson, J. D. 1980. Skewed floweirng distributions and pollinator attraction. **Ecology**, 61: 572-579.

Tohda, H. 1983. Seed morphology in Orchidaceae I. *Dactylorchis, Ponerorchis, Chondradenia* and *Galeorchis*. **Science Report Tohoku University** (4th ser.), 38: 253-268.

Tohda, H. 1985. Seed morphology in Orchidaceae. II. Tribe Cranichideae. **Science Report Tohoku University** (4th ser.), 39: 21-43.

Tohda, H. 1986. Seed morphology in Orchidaceae. III. Tribe Neottieae. **Science Report Tohoku University** (4th ser.), 39: 103-119.

Van Der Pijl, I. and Dodson, C.H. 1966. **Orchid Flowers, Their Pollination and Evolution**. Coral Gables: University of Miami Press.

Vance, B.D. and Kucera, C.L. 1960. Flowering variation in *Eupatorium*. **Ecology**, 41: 340-345.

Verma, J. C. and Sahno, K.C. 1976. Rare orchids of North-Eastern region and their conservation. **Ind. For.**, 102: 424-431.

Veyret, Y. 1974. Development of the embryo and the young seedling stages of orchids. In: C.L. Withner (ed.) **The Orchids: Scientific studies**, 223-265. John Wiley and Sons, NewYork, NY.

Vij, S.P. 1989. Chromosomes and specifation in Indian orchids. **J. Orchid Soc. India**, 3(1-2): 11-24.

Vij, S.P. 1998. Orchidology in India: Current status. In: **International festival of orchids** (ed. Dr. S.N. Hegde), pp. 1-11.

Vij, S.P., Arora, A. and Nanda, U.S. 1976b. In IOPB chromosome number reports. **Taxon**, 25: 631-649.

Vij, S.P., and Kashyap, S.K. 1978. Palynological studies in some Orchidaceae. **Abst. II. Ind. Palyn. Conf.**, Bangalore.

Vij, S.P. and Shekhar, N. 1986. Cytogenetical aspects of Indian orchids. In: Biology, conservation and culture of orchids (ed. S.P. Vij), pp. 189-220. Affiliated East West Press, New Delhi.

Vij, S.P., Shekhar, N., Kuthiala, R. and Sood, A. 1981. In: IOPB Chromosome number reports. **Taxon**, 30: 506-512.

Vij, S.P., Shekhar, N., Kuthiala, R. and Sood., A. 1983. In: IOPB Chromosome number reports. **Taxon**, 32: 138-41.

Vij, S.P. and Sood, R. 1986. Chromosome number in Indian orchids - A complete tabulation. In: **Biology, conservation and culture of orchid.** (ed. S.P. Vij) East-West Press, New Delhi. pp. 221-292.

Wadhwa, P.M., Singh, D.K. and Singh, K.P. 1990. A conspectus of orchids of Mizoram. Their status and conservation. **J. Orch. Soc. Ind.** 4(1,2): 51-64.

Waser, N.M. 1979. Pollinator availability as a determinant of flowering time in ocotillo (*Fouquicria splendens*). **Oecologia**, 39: 107-121.

Went, F.W. 1957. The plants of Krakatoa. In G. Piel *et al.* (eds.), Plant life - A scientific American book. pp. 137-145. Senion and Schuster, New York.

White, L.M. 1979. Relationship between meterological measurements in flowering of index species to flowering of 53 plant species. **Agri. Meteorol.**, 20: 189-204.

Wielgolaski, F.E. 1973. Phenology in agriculture. In: H. Leith (ed.), Phenology and seasonality modelling. Spring-er-Verlag, New York. pp. 369-381.

Wilcox, B.A. 1984. *In situ* conservation of genetic resources: Determinant of minimum area requirements. Proc. World National Parks Congress. Bali, Indonesia, Glant I.U.C.N.

Williams, N.H. 1970. Some observations on polliaria in the Oncidinae; **Am. Orch. Soc. Bull.**, 41: 207-220.

Williams, N.H. and Broome, C.R. 1976. Scanning electron microscope studies of orchid pollen. **Am. Orch. Soc. Bull.**, 45: 699-707.

Woodard, J.W. 1952. Some chromosome numbes in *Vanda*. **Am. Orchid Soc. Bull.**, 21: 247-249.

Wright, S.J. 1991. Seasonal drought and the phenology of understory shrubs in a tropical moist forest. **Ecology**, 72: 1643-1657.

Writh, M. and Withner, C.L. 1959. Embryology and development in the orchidaceae. In: **The orchids: A scienfitic survey** (ed. C.L. Withner). The Ronald Press, New York, pp. 155-188.

Wyatt, R. 1982. Inflorescence architecture: how flower number, arrangement, and phenology affect pollination and fruit set. **Am. J. Bot.**, 69: 585-594.

Wodehouse, R.P. 1935. **Pollen grains, their structure, identification and significance in science and medicine**. London.

Yeung, E.C. and Blackman, S.J. 1983. Floral biology and *Epidendrum ibaguense* H.B.K. I. Development of the pollinium. **Am. Orch. Soc. Bull.**, 52: 836-40.

Ziegler, B. 1981. Mikromorphologie der Orchideensamen unter Berucksichtigung taxonomischer Aspekte. Ph.D. dissertation, Ruprecht karls Universitat. Heidelberg.

Zimmerman, J.K. and Aide, T.M. 1989. Pattern of fruit production in a neotropical orchid: pollinator vs resource limitation. **Am. J. Bot.**, 76: 67-73.

# Appendix

### *Vanda thwaitesii*

At the time of writing of this work a species was reported. [Rheedea 8(2): 249–253. 1998). This species, was first collected by Thwaites from Sri Lanka. At the time it was wrongly placed as *Erides tessellatum* in 1861. J.D. Hooker (1898) renamed the species as *Vanda thwaitesii* when he came across its drawing and descriptions. As this species was not reported for 137 yrs. Jayaweera (1981) declared it as extinct.

Satish Kumar had collected this species from the Silent Valley in 1982. Later on it was collected for a numer of times from Northern Kerala. Due to its close resemblance with *V. tessellata* (Roxb.). W.G. Hook. ex. G. Don, the species was not considered to be different from it for a long time. Only after Dr. Eric Christinson confirmed it as the supposedly extinct species – *V. thwaitesii,* this species was studied and its details noted.


1. Sathish, C. and P.C. Suresh Kumar. The reappearance of *Vanda thwaitesii* J.D. Hook (Orchidaceae). Rheedea Vol. 8(2): 249–253. 1998.
2. Hookers J.D. 1898. Orchidaceae. In: H Trimen's Handbook of the flora of Ceylon 4: 193.
3. Jayaweera, D.M.A. 1981. Orchidaceae In: Dasanyake, M.D. & F.R. Fosberg (ed), A Revised Handbook to the flora of Ceylon Vol. 2: 230. New Amerind Publishing Co., New Delhi.

# Index

micronutrient deficiencies or excesses, making farm- level yields and aggregate production low and unstable. While half the area sown to wheat in developing countries and up to 70 percent of that grown in developed countries suffers from periodic drought, wheat has been found to be relatively drought hardy, unlike maize, which may fail completely if the flowering stage is delayed beyond a critical threshold due to drought.

Breeding for drought tolerance in wheat, therefore, should focus more on improving overall radiation use efficiency under stress rather than reproductive stages of growth and partitioning. In an Australian study, improved early vigorin wheat was also found to be an important trait for increasing water-use efficiency and thereby grain yields in rainfed environments, but only at a medium rainfall site. At drier sites, greater early vigor initiates terminal drought earlier to reduce yield.

Conventional varieties already exist that grow in dry upland fields but they cannot match the yield potential of conventional commercial varieties, nor do they respond to irrigation or fertilization. Weed growth that is normally suppressed by flooding but can be dominant on dry land is another challenge for aerobic rice. The biggest concern with the current varieties of aerobic rice is a "yield collapse," in which the harvest is acceptable in the first season but drops by about 20 percent in the second and may fall a further 70 percent in the third. Although the reason for this yield-collapse is unknown, experience shows that it doesn't occur when rice is rotated with other crops. Aerobic rice is grown commercially while rotating with other crops under irrigation on 250,000 hectares in Brazil.

#### *Desirable Traits*

Combining desirable traits such as increased biomass

production, stress tolerance, and quality traits such as cooking quality are becoming a common strategy of breeders. A major constraint to hybrid use, especially to resource-poor farmers, is loss of hybrid vigor if the next generation seeds are kept and used for the following season, forcing farmers to purchase seeds each season. One goal of breeders is to develop maize and rice varieties that will reproduce through apomixis, so that the seeds of a hybrid with this trait can be retained from one year to the next.

The ability to transfer apomixis capability to maize from its wild relative, Tripsacum (although it is admittedly difficult) represents an untapped genetic resource for abiotic and biotic stress resistance. Apomixis could greatly simplify the production of hybrid seeds and make it possible for farmers to buy seed of improved varieties at a much lower price. Some researchers estimate that the introduction of apomictic maize could reduce seed costs by at least 25 percent.

The breeding process involves increasing photosynthesis by inserting a 47 maize gene into the hybrid rice. This GM Fhybrid rice is expected to be ready for trial in 2004, and may be available to Chinese farmers by 2008. In the United States, RiceTech released XL6, the first Fhybrid rice variety for highly mechanized farming in January 2000. More than 180 farmers in Arkansas and Missouri planted XL6 on about 11,000 acres in 2001.

Cereal yield growth in farmers' fields will come both from incremental increases in the yield potential in rainfed and irrigated areas and from improved stress resistance in diverse environments, including improved drought tolerance (together with policy reform and investments to remove constraints to attaining yield potential, as discussed in the next section). The rate of growth in yields will be enhanced by extending research both downstream to farmers and upstream to the use of tools derived from biotechnology to assist conventional breeding, and, if concerns over risks can be solved, from the use of transgenic breeding.

Participatory plant breeding plays a key role for successful yield increases through genetic improvement in rainfed environments (particularly in dry and remote areas). Farmer participation in the very early stages of selection helps to fit the crop to a multitude of target environments and user preferences. Ceccarelli et al. demonstrate that participatory plant breeding may be the only possible type of breeding for crops grown in remote regions, a high level of diversity is required within the same farm, or for minor crops that are neglected by formal breeding.

Moving upstream, with the progress in mapping cereal genomes, the similarities between cereal crops will facilitate the integration of cereal genetic information and contribute to the faster identification of desirable traits. In order to assure effective breeding for high stress environments, the availability of diverse genes is essential. It is therefore essential that the tools of biotechnology, such as marker-assisted selection and cell and tissue culture techniques, be employed for crops in developing countries, even if these countries stop short of true transgenic breeding.

To date, however, application of molecular biotechnology has been limited to a small number of traits of interest to commercial farmers, mainly developed by a few life science companies operating at a global level. Very few applications with direct benefits to poor consumers or to resource-poor farmers in developing countries have been introduced-although the New Rice for Africa (NERICA) may show the way for the future in using biotechnology tools to aid breeding for breakthroughs beneficial to production in developing countries. Much of the science and many tools and intermediate products of biotechnology are transferable to solve high priority problems in the tropics and subtropics, but it is generally agreed that the private sector will not invest sufficiently to make the needed adaptations in these regions.

Consequently, national and internationa l public 49 sectors in the developing world will have to play a key role, much of it by accessing proprietary tools and products from the private sector. However, there has been little detailed analysis of the incentives and mechanisms by which such public-private partnerships can be realized. Most developing countries have virtually no capacity in molecular biology research, although strong programs exist in countries such as China, India and Brazil.

Development of GMOs also has significant potential for improving stress tolerance and yields in rainfed (and irrigated) environments, if concerns over consumer and environmental safety can be overcome. However, although cell and tissue culture and other agricultural biotechnology research are underway in many developing countries, most transgenic crops are planted in the developed world for developed country markets.

In 1999, North America accounted for 82 percent of genetically modified plantings, with the United States alone accounting for 72 percent. In Asia, only China has a significant area planted to GM crops. The first country in the world to approve commercialization of GM crops, China has authorized the environmental release of over 100 varieties, including insect resistant-cotton, virus-resistant tobacco, papayas, green peppers, and potatoes, and slow ripening tomatoes. India is undertaking major research, but has yet to approve the commercialization of GM varieties.

When biotechnology moves beyond the application of molecular biology to assist conventional breeding to the creation of transgenic crops, it may introduce risks associated with the release of genetically modified material into the environment. These risks could include genes 'jumping' from genetically modified plants to other plants through cross-pollination, rapid creation of new pest biotypes through adaptation to genetically modified plants, and allergic reactions to the consumption of genetically modified foods.

# Bibliography


Blair, Adam, "Supermarket Technology, The Big Picture." *Supermarket News,* February 23:p.1A-19A, 1999.

Byerlee, D., P. Heisey, and P. Pingali. "Realizing yield gains for foods staples in developing countries in the early 21st century: Prospects and challenges". *Paper presented to the Study Week on "Food Needs of the Developing World in the Early 21st Century,"* January 27-30, The Vatican, Italy, 1999.

Cai, X., and M. W. Rosegrant. "Irrigated and rainfed crop area and yield in China, India, and the US". *International Food Policy Research Institute,* Washington, D.C., 1999.

Critchley, W., and K. Siegert. Water harvesting: A manual for the design and construction of water harvesting schemes for plant production. Rome, Italy: *Food and Agricultural Organization of the United Nations,* 1991.

Habitu, N., and H. Mahoo. "Rainwater harvesting technologies for agricultural production: A case for Dodoma, Tanzania". *In Conservation tillage with animal traction,* ed. P.G. Kambutho, and T.E. Simalenga. Harare, Zimbabwe: A resource book of Animal Traction Network for Eastern and Southern Africa (ATNESA), 1999.

Hazell, P., and C. Ramasamy. "The green revolution reconsidered: The impact of high-yielding rice varieties in South India". Baltimore, U.S.A.: The John Hopkins University Press, 1991.

Heisey, P. W., M. L. Morris, D. Byerlee, and M. A. Lopez-Pereira, "Economics of hybrid Maize adoption". *In Maize seed industries in developing countries*, ed. M. L. Morris. Boulder, Colorado: Lynn Rienner Publishers Inc, 1998.

Kinsey, Jean and Sara Ashman, "Information Technology in Retail Food Industry," *Technology in Society*, 22:1, p. 83-96, 2000

______________, "Concentration of Ownership in Food Retailing: A Review of the Evidence about Consumer Impact," August, 1998. University of Minnesota, The Retail Food Industry Center, *Working Paper* 98-04, 1998.

Li, F., S. Cook, G. T. Geballe, and W. R. Burch Jr., "Rainwater harvesting agriculture: an integrated system for water management on rainfed land in China's semiarid areas". Ambio 29(8): 477-483, 2000.

Maredia, M. K., D. Byerlee, and P. Pee. "Impacts of food crop improvement research: Evidence from sub-Saharan Africa". *Food Policy 25* (2000): 531-559, 2000.

# Index